DISASTROUSLY FABULOUS

DISASTROUSLY FABULOUS
A Novel of Loves, Betrayals and New Beginnings

by D.A. Prince

Copyright © 2016 by D.A. Prince

Disastrously Fabulous

A Novel of Loves, Betrayals and New Beginnings

by
D.A. Prince

DEDICATION

·

Renee who always encouraged me to write a book -
finally, I am taking the challenge!

My parents who have been my rock and
who pick me up from every fall.

Many thanks to my wonderful husband
who has always been supportive.

My loving children, my best creation. They tell me how much
they love me every day. I love and appreciate my family
and am thankful to everyone for all you do.

To all who continue to have patience with me
working on evolving every day!

TABLE OF CONTENTS

THE FIVE LESSONS

*"Detach from needing to have things work out a certain
way. The universe is perfect and there are no failures. Give
yourself the gift of detaching from your worries and trust that
everything is happening perfectly."*

~ *Orin* ~

MY NAME IS CRYSTAL. I've been called a firecracker, a go-getter, a live wire. I have also been called less complimentary terms that rhyme with words like 'stitch' and 'score.' Alright, I can be a bitch! But that has never bothered me much. In my life, I learned nearly every lesson the hard way. I mean, in a really hard way.

If the hard way was a stone, mine would have been a diamond. "Your problems are diamond hard, so you might as well shine like Crystal," my dad would say in his lyrical Jamaican accent. That is how I got my name, and so my name turned out to be a reflection of the life that stretched out before me.

I like to think of it as disastrously fabulous, a beautiful succession of lessons that made almost no sense to me until I took the time to sit down and reflect. And what horrific pain it was! No one died – but the death of a lover and losing part of me each time with love, felt emotionally terrible.

When betrayed or lied to, no one can brace themselves for how they'll feel or react. Getting through heartbreak and heartache is tough. Especially as a young person; nothing prepares you if you've found love. Although, I did enjoy the Concord flights, celebrity parties… and the affluence.

Only a few people can say that they've had a taste of the lux life and then lost it all. That's how it felt at the time. Rarely have they seen what I have seen, or experienced what I have done. But this is hardly my story. In fact, it's a story about the five men who I have loved in my life and the lessons they taught me. Isn't love an incredible thing?

Most fascinating, I think, is how it can blind you to the circumstances of your life. Love, you see, has been my biggest and most persistent problem. I used to believe with every molecule of my heart that love could conquer anything. Well, girls, I had it a little wrong. Love can give you the world, but it can also rob you of it.

I'm proud that I've loved with such ferocity in my life. It took me everywhere I wanted to go. But again, I learned the real meaning of the term by living through it. With five broken hearts come five diamond memories, as well as the advice I know that you need or perhaps find helpful.

And so here I am with these *five lessons of love*. These diamond lessons brought to you by a woman that made every mistake in the book and survived with a smile on her face and love in her heart. What is real love? And what does it look like? Now I know what it's supposed to feel like. I have seen every lie and walked through the fire of every separation.

I'll show you how to sparkle like a Crystal, baby.

CHAPTER 1

DOMESTIC BLISS

*"True love is like ghosts, which everyone talks about and few
have seen."*

~ François de La Rochefoucauld ~

I HAD IT ALL. The gorgeous high-rise, New York Apartment on 48th Street, a Bentley limousine with a chauffeur to drive me around town, bedroom-sized closets brimming with Gucci dresses, Christian Louboutin shoes and Cartier jewelry. Light, harmony, and the fabulous life belonged to me. These were the things that made me feel great.

I figured it out, at last, this crazy roller-coaster ride called love. Burt was a sweet man—romantic, fun and oh so wealthy! I couldn't have asked for anything more wonderful. We were a power couple, a part of the African-American elite. My husband stormed Wall Street and made a fortune before he hit 35.

By the time I caught his eye, I was already part of the 'it crowd', working as a financial advisor in the Big Apple. At 34, with three children and a husband who would fly me around the world, I didn't have to worry about a thing. It was domestic bliss.

Of course, it was also one big, fat lie, like a sales item you bring back home, only to discover that the original price was a few hundred dollars less than what you just bought it for, Burt's idea of domestic bliss was different than mine.

That morning I woke up tired, still a little cloudy from our recent trip to Cabo with our twins and James. It was Saturday, more than enough time to recover properly before Burt headed back to work, and I busied myself with the girls, tennis, society life, and shopping.

Since marrying Burt, I no longer needed to work, so I ditched the financial service racket. It was never my passion, and it had served its purpose—to find me a good, stable man. Don't get me wrong, I am no gold digger. I've been with a variety of men. I just decided young that affluent men were more fun.

My aunt always used to tell me that with my looks, I could have anyone I wanted. I've been lucky in my life that this has been true for the most part. Burt was attracted to my beauty, but he fell in love with my attitude. He needed someone around to help spend his wealth on experiences that enriched our lives, and I was the woman to do it. It was an art.

By mid-morning the maid was attacking my luggage, three large bags that needed to be unpacked before the weekend was over. The twins were off visiting their father Max, and James was taking a nap in his bedroom. Travel can be exhilarating and exhausting all at once. I made a mental note to give the nanny a call; Burt wanted dinner at the country club that evening.

Most Saturday nights we drove out of the city to meet up with friends at The Monterey, an exclusive country club where Burt hosted a lot of his business deals. I was always the perfect wife, adding an element of fun and comfort to the competitive negotiation process. I'm magnificent at creating an ambiance.

"Dinner reservations are for six, babe." Burt pulled on his gym clothes and gave me that million-dollar smile. He could make my knees go weak, oh that man.

"Okay, hon, I'll get hold of Julie and let her know to be here by five. Are your bags unpacked yet?" I called as I disappeared around the corner, with an armful of clothes for the hamper.

"I'll get them done tomorrow. Today I need to focus on feeling good for this business meeting. I need to be on my game," he called after me as

I assisted the maid in dropping the clothes into our large laundry room, off our third master bathroom, adjacent to the kitchen.

He seemed agitated, but perhaps the meeting was playing on his mind. Burt could disappear into his work, which is what made him so successful. I pushed the feeling out of my mind and spent the next hour in one of my favorite places—my closet. It was a custom-built design wonder that rotated a full 360 degrees.

If I wanted something, I only had to search for it on the system. It was entirely digital and keeping it organized was a job all on its own—but I loved it. Like everything else in my life, I spent an inordinate amount of time making sure whatever I wore made an impact and pleased Burt. You have to keep your man, happy, right?

My gorgeous sapphire-blue dress with the draped shoulders and nipped waist would be perfect for dinner that evening.

Our trip to Cabo had been incredible. We stayed in plush luxury at a five-star hotel in the penthouse suite for the two weeks we were down in Mexico. The white sand beaches, tropical drinks, and azure blue waters were exactly what we needed for some serious downtime. I had worn the blue dress on our first evening there, and Burt had loved it.

My closet shuddered along soundlessly, speeding the spare blue dress towards me. I had purchased two of them at Barney's before we left on holiday because I liked it so much. I grabbed the dress and hung it on the dressing rack next to my all white furniture.

I turned on the stereo and let the music pump into the room. Music didn't soothe my soul so much as keep it alive. A good song could instantly transport me into the mind of a famous singer, and I could become Rihanna or anyone else I cared to be with the right props and enough alone time.

At four years old, James often sneaked into the room after me and switched up the music, just to watch me perform as each singer. I did a mean Michael Jackson, but I never really got the hang of Beyoncé... though I liked to think that it was because of my authentic performances. My voice was about as silky as a polyester scarf bought from Chinatown.

"You're growing up so fast, aren't you? My little man." My son was going to grow up to be a smooth dancer like his dad. We walked to the kitchen together, a marble palace of silver fixtures and the finest wooden finishes. I fixed us both my son's favorite, toasted grilled cheese, and we settled in front the television together.

Our television was the size of a small state and stretched from one side of the room to the other, like a fifth member of the family. Burt insisted that this television was the best, but sometimes I wondered. Was bigger better? I turned the stereo off and popped on some cartoons for James. He giggled manically as he watched.

The only sound I liked better than music was hearing my children laugh. I sat there for quite some time before I heard the creep and crackle of movement going on in the other bedroom. Burt must have finished his workout. James seemed happy enough, so I rose and silently glided over to the bedroom.

I peeked around the corner, and Burt was sitting on the bed. As silent as a nuclear test alarm, I dropped all presence when he looked up and fumbled around for a set of keys that was not there.

"Hey babe." He looked like a cat that has just had a league of his familiar feline colleagues sink their claws into his tail. "What's up?"

"What's up?" I repeated. Burt's voice never cracked that way, and I could feel the tension in the room rise. What was wrong? I settled on the bed next to him. "Isn't that my iPad, honey?"

He scooted backward some and continued to swipe through the iPad.

"What are you looking for?"

"Just looking at some photos from…from Los Cabo. I thought there may have been a few that I missed." He flopped the iPad down on the bed, the screen dark.

"That's weird. We spent the last five hours looking at the pictures on the flight home. You had the entire file on your phone."

"Anyway, I better jump in the shower. This meeting is getting to me and it's getting late." The words came out in a rushed way, and he wasn't meeting my eyes. "Better wash the stress away. You all set for tonight?"

Before I could answer, he clicked the door shut behind him. Moments later, the shower whooshed and steam filtered under the door.

My mind exploding into suspicion. What was going on?

Most men have secrets. But Burt was an upright man, and he rarely exuded such obvious discomfort.

I tried to stay rational, but my mind churned, as if James's cartoon had sprung to life, and the Opposite Day comedy was unfolding in real life.

Confusion gave way to a sense of impending doom. It was the kind of instinctive warning animals get when a tsunami is heading for the shoreline. Maybe I was still vibe-ing off that Rihanna song I'd listened to earlier. Still, inside me, something couldn't settle down. I sat frozen to the bed while the shower pattered down in the other room.

I reached for my iPad and turned it on: Los Cabo pictures.

But why would Burt want to look at them again? He had every copy of every photo. What was he looking for?

Then it struck me, as the jealous hand of fate whipped me across the face. Burt was suspicious of me. He was looking for evidence that I had done something wrong.

My previous relationships had taught me that the most jealous person in the relationship is usually the one who's doing something wrong. They are suspicious and insecure because they project their own behavior onto you.

The waters rolled out, and the wave grew enormous.

My head buzzing, I sank into a slow motion reaction. Rich men would always have busy bees fluttering around them to whom money was honey. But I had trusted Burt.

I stood and made my way over to his jacket, where his cell phone would be. It was easy. I dipped my hand into the pocket, and there it was. No password was needed; Burt didn't keep his phone locked— why would he? I had never checked it before. I trusted him. I returned to the bed, sitting cautiously with the phone in my hands.

I knew that once I crossed this line, I could never go back. That hidden in this phone might be answers to questions that could change everything. But it was already too late! I was a bloodhound, a greyhound, a heat seeking missile! My brain said no while my fingers worked against me.

The sounds of water and Sponge Bob Square Pants echoed through the lounge. My son just completed another hearty laugh and was cheering for his favorite character, Patrick. The phone felt strangely cold in my hands, foreign—like I was invading a defenseless country. I pushed the hesitation from my mind and broke in.

Burt was never jittery like that. Something was wrong. My brain knew it, my fingers knew it and my heart knew it. Even my closet knew it, as I mistakenly sat on my remote and it clattered to life. I paused briefly to turn it off again. The screen shone back at me, an index of faces, places, and names.

Where would a foreign country hide their secrets? I thought after browsing some random photos for a few minutes. Then I knew. They wouldn't hide them. They would delete them. But phones never really 'hard' deleted anything. Deleted files were always available if you knew where to find them.

Like a barbarian invading the Roman Empire, I stormed into Burt's deleted files. For a brief, shining moment, I convinced myself that my actions were innocent. That I didn't need to worry and all I would find there would be work texts and bad photos of our trip. Then I opened the first file. It was a picture of a vagina. Someone's disgusting pussy.

CHAPTER 2

A NIGHTMARE DURING THE DAY

"Sometimes it takes a heartbreak to shake us awake & help us see we are worth so much more than we're settling for."

~ Mandy Hale ~

WHEN YOU'RE FACED WITH the prospect that your husband is cheating, several things happen to you at once. You feel despair settle in your stomach, like lead. Your heart feels like melting ice cream, and no matter how hard you try you can't stop it slopping on the floor. Your head fills with moments of the past and everything becomes an insidious plot.

When you're faced with another woman's vagina, only one thing happens. That one thing manifested in me as a maniacal, twenty-minute hunt to find out who the lady parts belonged to. I needed to know.

But first, I had to swipe past the vaginal monster and search for more clues.

Boobs and bits, boobs and bits.

Whoever this woman was, she had a very high opinion of her sex organs. It would have made me sick to my stomach, but instead, it made me rage. I was the goddess of thunder, shaking in all of my thwarted beauty—thoughts of rampant murder itching in my fingertips.

Why couldn't I just have let it be! Why did I have to discover a virtual treasure trove of snatch? I sat staring at what I could only hope was this woman's most attractive feature, lost in a black mirage of fury. I started towards the shower door a few times, considering how easy it might be to bludgeon Burt with one of those ceramic pots he loved, or to drown him in his spa bath.

No woman who loves a man should ever have to discover something as outrageous as another women's penis fly trap on their phone. What kind of a woman was this? Did she get kicks out of debasing herself like a $5 hooker?

James was constantly playing on his father's apps. What if he stumbled across this whore of horrors?

"I'm going to kill him!" I thought savagely. "I'll hit him where it hurts. I hope he's enjoying his shower because it's the last time he'll be well enough to take one on his own."

It was the end. I knew it was. I would stay by a man's side through anything, but not through cheating. I respected myself far too much for that.

What outraged me the most was that I had suspected Burt of cheating since the beginning of the year. Things had not been the same since then. He'd become distant, like I lost a part of him. Now it was clear that he was giving that part to someone else. Hell-fire burned in my belly. I was so angry; the sheer heat of my hatred could have eviscerated that girl's vagina.

I imagined her at work, minding her own business, when suddenly - poof! No more lady bits. A spontaneous combustion that would serve her cheating ass right. She'd never hurt another woman with porn pics of her pussy again. This vicious fantasy kept me from imploding.

Burt would try to tell me these photos had just mysteriously appeared – but these weren't common dirty pictures circulating online featuring a porn model's improbable perfections. This was a real woman, with uneven boobs, someone he knew, someone he was involved with. I had to find out who, before Burt got out of the shower.

I clicked Burt's laptop into action and navigated to Facebook. It was password protected, but I could still log in with my account. I searched through photo after photo on his page, and lo and behold, a familiar image cropped up. I wasn't certain it was the same image, but the boobs were a match, with the left one bigger and much lower than the right, and an arrow-shaped mole under the collarbone matched too.

About two weeks before Los Cabo, Burt had been leaving comments on this woman's whack photos on Facebook. They seemed…overly familiar. Too many smiley faces, winks, and compliments. When I asked him about this, he'd laughed it off, and said it was just some woman working out in the same gym.

Now it seemed they'd been working out together in quite a different way.

My lying, cheating husband has been ogling another woman's honey pot. Something intimate was going on, and I was sure that the girl from the fitness club was involved.

I checked her name: Layaho.

For a few minutes, I entertained myself dreaming up ways I could teach that Layaho a lesson. I could still not fathom what kind of slut would send a married man such explicit photos. That bitch needed therapy. Or her face kicked in.

The bathroom door swung open, and steam poured into the room like at an ominous stage show. Burt was standing in the doorway with a fluffy white towel wrapped around his hips and a smell of eucalyptus shower gel.

He took in the scene of me sitting on the bed like a volcano about to erupt. "What's wrong with you?"

"I have one question for you, just one." My voice was dangerously calm.

His face fell. "Okay…"

"Does this pussy belong to this hoe?" I held up his cell phone and turned the laptop around.

"What? What are you talking about?"

"Are you cheating on me with this slut? Or have I somehow misinterpreted this friendly exchange of sex organs?"

"Just calm down, Crystal, we can talk about this." He closed the bathroom door. "Why are you looking at my phone?"

I stood, fuming. "You ask that, when a moment ago you were spying on mine? Answer my question. Is it hers?"

"Crystal, those are just photos, alright," he started. "It's not what you think, I swear." His voice sounded strained as he groped for excuses.

I was not interested in hearing lies. "Just stop it, Burt. When did you stop loving me? How can you lie to me like this and cheat on me with this skank?" I threw his phone at him.

"Oh get a life, Crystal, I'm not doing anything to you. Look at you, searching through my private phone for something to be mad about. I have to get ready for my meeting, and now I have to deal with this shit?" He was getting upset. Burt was never any good at being upset; he always tended to overreact.

"Who is that, Burt?" I demanded. "That is not just some porn you got off the Internet. That's a real person, someone you know. Who?"

"I told you, I don't know who that is—I can't help it if women send me dirty photos. I get them often and I delete them; you can see that!"

"They are in your temporary deleted files; you are keeping them!"

"That's not true." He pulled on his sharp-creased trousers without looking at me.

"Don't just ignore me, Burt. Women don't send photos like this to men with whom they aren't involved."

He buttoned up his crisp white shirt. "This crazy woman does."

"Oh, so you do know her, you know exactly who she is! And she sends photos of her nasty tits and bits to everyone, does she?"

Burt clearly thought I was an idiot he could placate with lies. He meant to lull me back into submission by insisting he had better things to do than fight. "Look, Crystal, nothing is going on, alright! I commented on a friend of mine's Facebook photos and some girl sent me nude pictures. It happens."

His blasé attitude was churning me up. The violence inside wanted to peep its head outside to search harder for the truth.

"Stop lying to me! Why can't you just admit that you have been cheating? I have all the evidence I need here!" I was desperate. Had I lost perspective? Was this really just a crazy lady sending everyone pictures of her cooch?

No, no, no! It echoed inside me like a scream in an empty cavern. Men like Burt didn't get to do whatever they wanted just because they felt like it. This was crossing the line. I wouldn't be disrespected.

"What about you and Max?" Burt challenged. "I've seen your emails."

"Oh yes, turn it around on me. Typical! Max is Jordan and Joyce's father. There's nothing there, you know that!"

The argument heated and I could hear that someone turned up the cartoons in the lounge. The nanny must have arrived for James. Good thing too, as I suspected that things were about to kick off. I would get the truth out of Burt, even if it killed me.

"I know that you spend a lot of time with him, and that you are probably cheating on me. Anyway, you have never been able to control your mouth or your temper. Look at this mess… right before my meeting…" Burt was fully dressed now and was reaching for his Nordstorm leather slip-ons.

"If you mention your meeting again, hon, I'm going to lose my shit!" I sat on the bed, and calmly pulled the laptop onto my lap. I downloaded the file Ugly_Ass_Vagina_1 onto his desktop. I was going to post it on Facebook for everyone to see.

"What are you doing?"

"This fucking hoe likes to send everyone photos of her vagina, so I am going to help her advertise it! There! Now Facebook can enjoy everything her dirty ass has to offer." I clicked 'post' and it went live.

Burt flushed with frustration and anger. He was pissed off that I posted his girlfriend's pieces online. That was the moment I knew. Had these been a stranger's body parts, he wouldn't have cared.

"That's great, Crystal, really? Really mature response to this situation. Here let me make it clear for you…" He picked his phone up off the floor, and a second later the photo got a like on Facebook.

"You liked the photo?" I said, hurt to my core. "How could you do this to me?"

"That's what you get if you are always going to behave like a crazy bitch. I told you I wasn't cheating. I told you what happened, but you just can't accept it, can you?" Burt boomed. "I don't need this right now. You can stay here and deal with it. I'm out."

Burt grabbed his light jacket, leather briefcase and phone, and stormed out of the room, slamming the door behind him. Another banged door and he was gone.

He left, I kept thinking. A business meeting is more important than me.

The previous night, I'd enjoyed a romantic evening with Burt, fresh from our restful holiday in Los Cabo. And now this?

Cheating caused all these hard feelings, but he wouldn't admit to it. All I had were those nude photos, a gut feeling, a blurred image of a mole that might or might not be arrow-shaped, and Burt's behavior.

My thoughts careened around my head. I considered going down to the fitness club and talking to this Layaho to find out what was going on. But if she really was the skank, and she had seen me circulate her private parts in public, she would refuse to talk to me. Also, if she was the one, I had no desire to get close to her, except maybe to rake my nails across her face.

Burt's behavior was the most reliable clue to what was going on. It gave me the answer I needed, told me what Burt denied. His mouth said no, but his actions said yes. You cannot lie your way out of your own feelings. Burt was involved with that vagina, whoever she was. And he was angry with me for posting it on a public network.

Ironically, it was the act of posting it that kept me from breaking down. I achieved a victory, no matter how small. That would teach them to mess with my heart.

CHAPTER 3

GET A LIFE

*"If you live long enough, you'll make mistakes. But if you
learn from them, you'll be a better person. It's how you handle
adversity, not how it affects you. The main thing is never quit,
never quit, never quit."*

~ William J. Clinton ~

I WAS LEFT THERE, PERCHED on my percale cotton bedspread, surrounded by everything I could ever want in the world except the one thing I felt I deserved; real love. All Burt could say to me was 'get a life.' Did he really delude himself into thinking I didn't have one? I lived for him and our family. Now, once again I faced a choice.

I stared out of the top floor windows looking out over the city. Rectangular buildings, square ones, pyramid shapes, with dark dots for windows, and between streams of pin-prick cars. So many people, so much life!

How had I arrived in this situation? I'd always had a knack for inviting the entitled kind of men into my life. Selfish men who felt powerful. I chose to spend my life with them, instead of 'getting' my own.

ware of it, knew I sacrificed my career for love, made the choice many women make. When all of the wealth and power one side of the relationship, things generally tend to go south. Somehow I had convinced myself that Burt would be different from e previous men in my life. But he wasn't different at all—he was the same, and on top of that, he was an attention-seeking bastard.

This situation could be disastrous, because I had nothing to fall back on. Leaving Burt meant having to start over.

In this situation, some women would choose to stay. They would put up with their husbands misbehavior as the price to pay for the lifestyle. But I wasn't like that. I had a heart, and it beat for the man in my life. The relationship mattered more than the material comforts. It was always that way, since I was a young girl.

Like many serial cheaters with ways and means, Burt clearly didn't feel he had done wrong.

I sobbed with my face in my hands. I was older now and had become wiser. I made yet another mistake that would lead me back down the road to instability and sparseness. I understood myself though, and I could never be with Burt again.

Having to start over again was a major blow. I had no career, few qualifications and three kids. My only material asset was a condo apartment that I rented out. I should have done more when opportunity presented itself.

But this had always been my biggest strength and my most persistent weakness. I was amazing at living in the moment, having fun and enjoying life, and terrible at planning for the future. I had neglected myself, and now I had to stew in that neglect.

"The fifth time," I said aloud, horrified at my own bad luck. "I fell in love five times, and none of them worked out." Confusion spun a scarf of thoughts that draped over my mind. I felt cold and hot, enraged and in despair. Broken. Again. Enough was enough!

Where had I gone wrong?

My mother and father were both from Jamaica in the West Indies, and they had me when they were in their early twenties. My dad, Valentine, was a tall, broad man who would tower over most people, but the size of his body was nothing compared to the size of his heart.

My mother, Adel-jean, was his perfect complement, more creative and even-tempered than he was. The two of them worked to build a life together for their children, all ten of us. "Real love has a way of creating more family members," my mother would tell me.

Back home in Kingston, my father had grown in impoverished circumstances. His mother raised him single-handedly, and his alcoholic father was rarely around. The only good memories he had of his dad were after a few days of being with him. Some people make you happy when they are around; others make you happy when they leave, I guess.

In Jam Town, Jamaica, it was not uncommon to have a lot of brothers and sisters. My father had twelve other siblings from Grandma Doris, and she did just fine teaching each of them about the world and how to live in it.

The threat of extreme poverty scared my parents. They had a severe attitude when it came to money and practiced tough frugality. We never had enough money, and we the children had to start work as soon as we were able.

We always had food, a roof over our heads and clothes, but little else. Yet while poor in material things, but we were rich in love.

As a child, I was surrounded by love and acceptance. There was never a dull moment at our house.

We were poor, but my aunts and uncles were always around when we were growing up, bringing us things and having fun. They knew how to live life, and embrace every moment, regardless of their circumstances.

My aunt eventually helped my parents to come over to America where they started their family, and so we became citizens of the USA.

Had my parents attitudes towards money influenced my decision to marry wealthy men? It must have. For a young woman who had never experienced the finer things, even small gifts seemed like overwhelming gestures.

I often observed how rarely rich people had large families. They could afford to support many children, yet they chose to have only one or two children. Were they afraid the kids would squander their wealth?

My father was a great role model for me. A proud man who always worked more than one job at once, he taught me the value of having a good sense of humor. "Either you laugh at yourself, or the world will laugh at you," he used to tell me, "and there is nothing more painful than weaponized laughter."

We lived in Long Island, New York for a long time, as happy as a family could be that didn't have much. My mother spent all of her time looking after my ten brothers and sisters, and I learned the value of sharing at a very young age.

We knew the value of the US dollar, and what it meant to a large family like ours. Burt, however, didn't have that kind of mindset. The more he spent, the more there seemed to be.

"It's not whether you spend or not," he used to tell me, "but what you choose to spend it on."

Burt learned that investing was a sure-fire way to make a lot of money, and he solidified his wealth by always spending a large portion of it on more investments.

Beep. A text message jolted me back to the present. It was Burt.

"Hey babe. I've had lunch with this woman a few times, but we haven't slept together. I would never do that to you. She sent me those photos by mistake, (apparently she sent them to everyone on the Wi-Fi network at The Tasting Lounge) they were meant for her boyfriend. I hope we can sort this out. I love you. Burt."

A new story. Why did cheaters always think that once they were caught a new story would somehow exonerate them? Burt obviously didn't grasp that I had a ton of experience with cheaters. I knew exactly how men operated. First comes the denial, then comes the new story.

I bet he called that woman and they came up with it together. If I called her, their stories would align. But I'm not naïve like that anymore. If he had told the truth, they all would have pictures on their phones of the monster vagina. Burt probably thought I'd be too ashamed to call the restaurant. However, love has nothing to do with shame.

I Googled the number and called right away. "Yes, hello. I'd like to speak to your manager about a sensitive subject please."

A cheery tune jingled, then the line clicked. "Hello, this is Rachel."

Phew, a woman. This would be easier than I had thought. "Yes, hi Rachel. My name is Crystal. I have a strange question to ask you, and I would like you to keep it in confidence please."

"Of course, ma'am, how can I help?"

"You have a Wi-Fi network at your establishment?"

"Yes." I could hear the curiosity in her voice.

"Has any of your staff recently, say over the last month, received nude photos from a customer's phone by mistake?" I asked with confidence.

"Nude photos? No ma'am, nothing like that." She sounded confused.

"Are you sure, Rachel? I'm checking because my husband is claiming that the photos on his phone originated from a mass message on your network."

"I'm sorry to hear that, ma'am, but I can assure you than none of our staff have received any nude texts from our Wi-Fi connection at work. I hope this helps you settle the matter."

I thanked her. My heart sank a little lower. My last hope of an innocent mistake had gone, but I was not surprised, knowing that Burt was grasping at straws—his story was full of holes.

I responded to him.

"Hi Burt. Just called the restaurant. You are lying to me again. No one has ever received any nude photos there. Why not try honesty? Time to come clean."

My hands were shaking – not from nerves, but rather from emotional adrenaline. My body kept from breaking down by sending fresh waves of alertness through my brain.

Burt was an idiot. I might have bought that crap if I was ten years younger. I had bought into some bad lies in the past, and each of the man I had fallen in love with had brought poignant lessons.

Now Burt was about to become another lesson. I flopped down onto the bed and closed my eyes. Once again my thoughts landed on my childhood. I needed to understand what had gone wrong again. The only way to do that was to remember.

I grew up as a reasonably happy child. My parents were both loving and supportive, but I always had a sense that there was more to life than scrimping and saving.

My grandmother didn't approve of my mother and father's marriage. It caused contention in the family for quite some time. But there was no ignoring it—they were soul mates. All around me my friends' parents divorced, but not mine. They belonged together. They knew what it was to love and struggle as one, and I admit—I always wanted that.

And so I entered childhood with unrealistic notions of love.

CHAPTER 4

LIFE IN LONG ISLAND

"I spent my whole childhood wishing I were older and now I'm spending my adulthood wishing I were younger."

~ Ricky Schroder ~

As young children my siblings and I started out as Brooklyn locals, living in a two-bedroom apartment not fit for a family of our size. "It's small, but at least I can keep an eye on you troublemakers," my mother used to joke, peering at us over her morning newspaper. Our school was just across the road, but that only made us late every morning.

That apartment block was well kept and clean; nothing luxurious but it was home. With only two entrances it was our perpetual playground. We screamed around the hallways in our roller skates, knocking on our neighbors' doors then vanishing from sight. When you have nine siblings, a simple game like that can quickly turn into a disaster—everyone wants their turn.

We were those rowdy Jamaican kids from 3F, and proud of it. Despite our circumstances, there was always laughter and fun in our home. If one of the kids was not back for dinner by 5 o'clock, my mother walked the eight flights of stairs to the incinerator room below where our neighbors sometimes trapped various members of my family. Payback, I think, for the gross harassment of having kids knocking on your door just for fun.

"Dang it, how many times do I have to tell you kids not to skate in here! You're like mice that keep coming back for the cheese," my mom would say, releasing us from our temporary prison.

"It is good exercise though, Mommy," we replied with fits of laughter. Sometimes my brothers got trapped there just to hear my mom grumble about it. She never realized what we were up to.

We all went to Coney Island to the beach one weekend, and brought back a bag full of live crab.

Always up to mischief—and realizing that crabs were not very compliant or fun playmates—we smashed them with a hammer on the kitchen floor, to my mom's horror. Then, we were off to bed for what was supposed to be a lovely, fright-free evening. That was the first time I learned that crabs are pretty tough, and they seek revenge when you smash them.

As we were sleeping that night in our usual arrangement, me and my two sisters on a queen-sized bed—a half dead crab scuttled under the door into our room. I woke to my sister's scream of terror as it made a beeline for our pillows. That crab didn't survive the second attack wave, but we acquired a lot more respect for crabs after that.

Then, one morning, our Brooklyn paradise came to an end. We woke to the sounds of vigorous packing and a shocking announcement—we were moving to Long Island. Far removed from the inner city, Long Island was a small, middle class suburb in New York where my father managed to find us a three-bedroom home with a basement.

The glee on my parent's faces put us all at ease, but we were sad to leave. Our lives had been in Brooklyn. I said goodbye to my best friend, and an important part of my childhood—and we headed to our new suburban lives, far from the trappings of inner city poverty, crime and mischief.

As it turns out, my dad found us a nice, middle class house, surrounded by nice middle class people who smelled of lavender and hairspray. We didn't like them. My siblings and I were suspicious of how well-behaved everyone was. Plus, the move came with sacrifices. My father had always been frugal, but now he was counting pennies like an insomniac counts sheep.

Yet somehow, he managed to keep it light and cheery despite the sacrifices he made to move us there.

"Can we have money to go to the movies, Dad?"

"What? Movies? Why would you want to go to the movies when you have cable? Your own private luxury television, no strangers around to interrupt the story and all the popcorn you can eat? Forget going to the movies...the fun's right here!"

That man could make a dollar stretch like it was rubber. "Don't you worry about that movie; we will make our own theater experience tonight." And he always did. Even though we didn't have what others kids had, we never felt like we were missing out.

Moving to Long Island was an adjustment for all of us. It took me a while to realize that the kids there were not overly fond of immigrants. The friends I made didn't come from stable homes; most of their parents were divorced. This further entrenched the idea of love and solidarity in my mind because of my parents.

When our first Christmas in Long Island arrived, my siblings and I wanted nothing more than a Christmas tree. Our hearts were set on a tall, towering tree we could decorate together and stand in the living room of our new house, like any other family on the block.

We summoned up the courage to ask my dad, and, in his usual frugal spirit he gave us what we wanted without having to spend so much as a dollar.

"A Christmas tree?" he said, surprised that we were asking, "Our yard is full of them! We must have five or six of them out there. Pick the one you like best and we will decorate it later on."

"But dad, can't we have one for inside?" we begged in unison.

"It's not necessary to kill the tree to enjoy it. If we leave it outdoors, we can use it again next year."

And that was that. We gathered in the snow later that evening as the sun was starting to sink in the sky. We hung tinsel and a few brightly colored Christmas balls on some of the heavy pine branches of the tree. Each of us took turns to add a decoration, and afterwards we stood back and admired our handiwork.

It was the most authentic Christmas tree I have ever decorated in my life. All the store-bought trees at the most expensive stores couldn't replace the brilliance of that one. The next morning, it was covered in snow—and we noticed some of the costlier Christmas decorations had been ferreted back inside by my father.

It didn't matter, the tree looked wonderful outside of our home that Christmas—the colors peeking out from the snow, the tree broad and leafy, completely unaffected by our offerings of shiny paper and cardboard cut-outs. My mother and father were always the lights in our home, so we didn't need any for the tree. That, and my father insisted that there was a perfectly good street lamp lighting the decorations a few feet away. We sang Christmas carols at the tree on Christmas Day and for the first time since we left Brooklyn, we felt at home.

School in Long Island was something of a culture shock. Our new middle class lives were challenging enough without encountering some of the hostility from other students for our 'foreign' status. It always blew my mind how silly this was—the only difference between them and me was when our families immigrated to America.

Everyone, in some way or another, was from somewhere else. It was hard enough being black in a new country, but with our obvious Jamaican accents, there was no hiding where we came from. I learned to ignore the whispers and the stares in the hallway until the novelty wore off and the kids found someone else to talk about.

One of the most glaring differences was how African-Americans threw the word 'nigga' around. Used as a term of endearment and used often, it was a strange word to hear when in our Jamaican home—it was never used at all. I couldn't help but find it offensive, as did all of my siblings when we started to make friends.

I never got used to hearing it, even when the rise of rap music in the nineties made it the most popular and commonplace term to use in certain circles, and found it mildly offensive, even when it was used casually by close friends. There were better words available in the English language to express fondness and unity.

The black community in Long Island didn't care about our opinions, of course, and so we fell in line, made friends and generally sought out mischief wherever it was hiding. It didn't take my sisters and I long to realize that if we wanted to fit in, we needed to stand out. This became a particular problem for us, because our father never had any extra money.

Fashion was important for popularity, and so we learned how to shoplift items from our local stores. At the end of the day after school, we visited different shops in the area, sneakily boosting them of their goods. How else were we going to look fly? With so many siblings, items of clothing were recycled more times than they could survive.

My parents would have killed us if they ever found out what we were doing. Our teen years in Long Island were eventful and lean, peppered with plenty of misadventures and common teen mistakes. My sister and I figured out a system that we could use if we wanted to sneak out to parties.

My mother, trusting as she was, expected us to do well at school, to always have our homework done and to pass all of our classes. This expectation was supported by my father, who often exploded into long-winded rants about 'American opportunity' and getting ahead here. Both my parents expected us to take the opportunities we were given so that we could make better lives than they experienced back in Jamaica.

It was a great idea, but it meant that my mom didn't bother to check on us very often. It was assumed that were always trying our best and working to be better. This left room for me and my sister and me to sneak out at night to see our friends, or to go to parties wherever they were happening. We hid in the bushes, waiting for my mom to leave for work so that we could run inside, clean up and get to school.

"Shh! Shhh! She's coming!" my sister would say and silence would fall on our hiding spot. We would track Mom until her car disappeared out of the driveway and we were in the clear.

"I am so not going to school today, I'm still a little drunk," I would tell my sister. We rushed upstairs and cleaned up, and were never caught.

There was something about hiding in a bush, and going out to parties at night that made us feel clever. Breaking the rules was fun.

"Do you think Mom will ever catch us?" I asked my sister one day.

"No, she's always too busy rushing off to work—she trusts us. And Dad goes to manage the buildings so early that we actually don't have to come back until after school, if we wanted. But we mustn't skip school too often or we will totally get busted."

Long Island probably never experienced anything like us before!

CHAPTER 5

MODELING TIMES

"One of the things that fascinated me about modeling was that you had the freedom to look any way you wanted."

~ Veronica Webb ~

HIGH SCHOOL STARTED GETTING easier for me, because I bloomed into a beautiful young woman.

"You can have anyone you want, Crystal," my aunt assured me. "Pick a good one."

Boosting was not a permanent solution to my financial problems, so I took on a job that I knew I could do well—modeling.

I took on part-time modeling gigs and discovered I had a gift: the power to pose. I got regular jobs and enjoyed myself, but my options were limited because I wasn't the specific type in demand at the time.

While still studying, I got a second job that I could do in conjunction with my modeling career. Through an employment agency, I secured work with music companies – first in the marketing department, then as the executive assistant.

I had grown up listening to hip hop legends like Public Enemy, LL Cool J and Run DMC, The Beastie Boys, and now I was meeting some of the big names in the hip hop business as part of my job.

It was a fun office to work in, and being around ambitious people made me want to do better in my own life. I hustled back then, attending castings, working hard at the office job and studying where I could. I loved every day.

But I was still a student as well as a part-time model, and couldn't give the job the commitment and competence my employers expected, so the good times came to an end.

However, I had caught my first glimpse into a life less ordinary, and I was hooked. As rewarding as my modest childhood had been, I was suddenly aware of all we missed out on because we didn't have much. Money, it seemed, was the thing that mattered most.

My aunt had started a fashion business in Jamaica, specializing artfully distressed denims. Her enterprise was a success, and the Nearly Yardy became a must-have brand.

Modeling the Nearly Yardy outfits got me the attention of a big modeling agency, and soon I got bigger and bigger jobs.

But I wanted more. I was drawn to the spotlight, to people with wealth and power. I wanted to be one of them, and I set out to achieve this.

My looks would open many doors for me. People treated me with respect, as if I knew a secret hidden from the rest of the world. "There's something about you girl," they told me on set, "whatever 'it' is, you got it." I decided to make the most of it.

Modeling gave me access inside exclusive events and to incredible people. Being good in front of a camera helped me to feel confident. Every time I was scheduled for a shoot, I was energized for days, tripping from the attention and the adrenaline of being great at something that was what most think of as easy. I was a natural.

When I spoke to impressive people, I learned how to casually name-drop and elevate my status in their eyes. This, combined with a bubbly personality and great looks was really all it took to find myself among some of the most influential people of our generation.

Being around musicians and superstars made me feel like that life was not only possible, but probable if I worked hard at it. I was in the right place at the right time. The Big Apple. The City of Dreams. It was in front of me, and I watched as it glided by.

In high school I was one of the super cool kids. Then, I graduated. Like most kids my age I had no idea who I wanted to be in the world. I knew that I wanted wealth and success. I was not yet sure how I would go about getting it.

So, the day after my high school graduation I sat down at our glass table where Dad was sifting through some paperwork while eating his favorite dish, oxtail with rice and peas.

"Dad? Can I talk to you?" I asked.

His eyes flicked up from the page he was signing in black pen. "Sure baby girl, I could use a break from these infuriating tenants."

My father's favorite pastime was complaining about the state of some of the buildings he managed in Brooklyn. His tenants there all paid late, trashed the apartments and were not fit to live in a cardboard box, in his opinion. "They don't know how good they have it," he often said.

That afternoon I was after real-world advice. My head was full of dreams, and my heart was full of joy. But high school was over, and I had no idea what to do with my time.

"School's done now," I started. "I have to decide what I am going to do. I thought that maybe I could go to college and study something."

He surveyed me over his glasses. "Few people are sure at your age. Why do you want to go to college, when you can get a job right away?"

"I thought that college might give me better opportunities," I said feebly.

"To do what? Earn money? Child, you just need to get a job for that. Do you know what you want to study?" he asked.

"No."

"Then I suggest you get some life experience first. You are young. If you want to study, then you should. But you'll have to earn it for yourself."

"So I should get a job right away?"

He put his pen down. "Crystal, there is no point studying when you don't know what to study. You are an adult now. You need to find yourself work. Once you have a job and a better idea what you want, you'll be able to save for the right studies. You and your ten siblings will all have to make your own way in the world."

What he said made sense. With so many sons and daughters, my father wouldn't be able to provide a college education for us all. Whatever happened in our lives would be up to us! My parents had brought us this far—my father was clear on that message.

Now it was about the decisions that I made. Unfortunately, being an impulsive teen also made me a poor decision-maker. I was not prepared for the world or anything in it. I had to teach myself to survive.

Following my father's advice, I took a permanent job in a furniture company where the sales floor smelled of artificial air freshener and piped music chirped relentlessly.

The uniform I had to wear was stiff and unflattering, and I felt like someone had stuffed me into a pillowcase. Whenever I tried to spruce up the look with a scarf, a brooch or other personal touch, the manager told me off.

The job was boring to the point of soul-destroying, but I worked extra hard to make the furniture buying experience was exciting for my customers.

I refused to let the dull drudgery dim my light, but looked forward to the day when I would be able to leave. Either I would move up through the ranks, save money and eventually go to college, or I would get a big break as a model. I was still doing modeling gigs on the side. That flame burned bright in me, and I was ready to jump at the first sign of success.

Every day my positive attitude expanded, and my confidence grew. In that soul-destroying place I found a way to see the light in the darkness. I could sparkle wherever I was. Then one day, destiny came knocking.

A tall, dark and handsome man noticed me from across the salesroom floor.

I didn't know it yet, but he would become my first lesson in love.

CHAPTER 6

MY FIRST KINDA LOVE

"My first love, I'll never forget, and it's such a big part of who I am, and in so many ways, we could never be together, but that doesn't mean that it's not forever. Because it is forever."

~ Rashida Jones ~

THAT LYING PLAYER BARRY was a tough lesson to learn. I was a teen, fresh out of high school and working my first dismal, disappointing job when he strode confidently into my life.

At more than 6 foot, Barry was a tall Nigerian man with brown skin and dark eyes. He was quite a bit older than me, but not so old that I didn't find him instantly attractive from across the salesroom floor.

I looked up, and there he was, staring right at me with his penetrating eyes. There was something alluring about his gaze. He held himself with such confidence and swagger than even I had to look away after a few seconds.

Barry looked like a cross between an underwear model and an African prince. If that wasn't enough, the moment he saw me he cut off the salesman off he was talking too, excused himself, and approached me instead.

He took my hand in both of his. "Pleasure to meet such a blooming flower in such an unexpected place." I giggled like a school girl. He reminded me of the music industry types, with his clean white shirt, a sports jacket and expensive slacks. I could instantly tell that he was rich!

I flushed at his charm and touch. "Can I help you with something?"

"You surely can. I would like to buy many things, and then perhaps take you on a date this evening?" He leaned down and kissed my hand. I inhaled his aftershave – something luxurious with notes of sandalwood and musk. It was done.

That day he spent several thousand dollars on furniture and appliances, giving me a hefty commission to match. We set a date for that night, but nothing could have prepared me for what was about to happen. Until that point, I was an inquisitive middle class Jamaican girl trying to work my way through life.

I had tasted wealth through the people I met, but never directly experienced it for myself. I rushed home to tell my sisters all about the African prince I met at Seaman's. He was going to pick me up at 8 o'clock, and sent me a message telling me to "dress up."

I was screaming inside, while my sisters were screaming on the outside. I tore off my work uniform and dumped it on the floor. He wouldn't see me in that stiff sack again.

I tried on dress after dress.

"Chill," my sisters advised me. "He's not going to take you to Red Lobster."

At last, I settled on a sheer number that was classic and classy.

A knock on my bedroom door some time later, and I was ready. It was my mother. "There is a very enthusiastic and charming gentleman outside in a limousine for you, Crystal," she said.

My sisters squealed in excitement, huddled around the front window, peering out to see him and the limo he drove in.

I greeted him, and his eyes lit up. When he took my hand, his grip was warm and confident. Together we walked to the white stretched limo, where the driver opened the door for me.

That evening we drank exquisite French champagne in the limo before we even arrived at the restaurant—an exclusive spot reserved for the rich and famous only. They greeted him like they knew him well.

More than that, because I was with him they treated me like royalty, even though I was wearing clothes from Walt Whitman Mall. Barry made me feel like the center of the universe, like I was the most special, unique and extraordinary woman he ever met. The impact of this was that everyone around us treated me the same way. I quickly fell in love.

At dinner that night, we spoke about many things. I was too young and too enamored by his attentions to realize that I should have been paying more attention to the things he was not telling me. "I am a businessman in the sales trade, but I also procure rare items for wealthy clients," he said over another glass of the rare Dom Pérignon champagne.

Barry was an impressive man. I took in everything he said so completely that I didn't stop to question any of it. I am sure now that Barry adored that about me. "Tell me about yourself," he said as our Kobe beef fillet arrived. All of my initial shyness fell away, after being marinated in the godly broth of champagne and shots.

"I've been modeling for a few months, and working with my aunt's growing fashion brand. Nearly Yardy, you may have heard of it." I tried to sound like I did indeed have some life experience.

Barry was a good listener and a smooth talker.

He turned everything into an opportunity to flirt and flatter. "Why have you taken a job at a furniture company?" he asked me, a broad smile on his face. "Surely a beauty like you doesn't belong there."

"I'm just trying to get along until my modeling career takes off," I told him. "My parents didn't have the funds to send me to college, so I decided to get a job and save for it myself. Though… truthfully, I have no idea what to study."

"I understand. I am a self-made man. A few years ago, I didn't know what to do with my life either."

Barry ordered us the third bottle of champagne, which blew my mind. How precious was this guy? "The trick is to do what you are good at. I am good at selling things. you'll find out what you are good at one day. In the meantime, you don't have to rush it. In Nigeria, a beauty like you would never have to work a day in her life."

That night was a fairy-tale. It changed my perception on what my life could be. I always dreamed of falling in love with a romantic man—but a rich, romantic man was a new idea completely. I was on the inside of something great, and I never wanted it to end.

He was the perfect gentleman and dropped me off at home in the limo. I spent that night telling my sisters all about him and the magical evening we enjoyed together. For the first time since working at Def Jam, I felt alive.

Barry was my first intoxicating love. Romance quickly sprang up between us and we saw each other more and more often. He would often send his limo to drive me around, and I felt like a queen in New York.

Each time I saw him, it would get better. Barry was the kind of man that always got what he wanted, but was also very private about his business dealings. Barry often got up and disappeared to talk on the phone, or would randomly leave a dinner for an hour or so. It didn't matter. When he returned he always made it up to me—things were intense.

Barry made sure that he lavished me with attention, gifts and the best of everything. He gave me so much that I dedicated all my time to making him happy. I learned fast that he loved to have fun, and so I became the central source of that fun. Wherever we went, we did it with a carefree attitude. Money was never an objection, and so there were no limitations. It was the most exciting thing I ever experienced.

About my job, I cared less and less. My performance suffered, and when my company was forced to downsize, I was the first they fired. I was glad to go. My teenage brain was filled with nothing but thoughts of Barry and the next time we would be together.

The point arrived where we decided to travel, and now that my job was not holding me back, I could do whatever I wanted. He took me on lavish trips to California, Beverly Hills, Maryland, and Washington DC. We traveled to Lagos, Nigeria, which was an absolute adventure.

I had found my one true love, or so I thought, convincing myself and that the dream was our lives would never end. He was happy as long as he was the center of my world. I gave Barry everything, my time, my love and my body. I believed in him, and I dreamed of the day when he would propose and my life would be perfect.

Barry supported my delusions. He was a master at making me feel like the most desired woman in the world. We spoke of true love, of marriage and of running away together. This was my first experience with being swept off my feet by a man. It wouldn't be my last but it was the benchmark for future encounters.

Soon, I was spending Barry's money for him, and he loved it.

It was a whirlwind, and toxic. We did everything in excess. That should have been a red flag for me. Instead I made excuses when things didn't seem or feel right. I wanted the romance with Barry to last forever.

If we got married, I wouldn't have to work, I'd focus on college and he would pay for it. Or even better, I didn't have to go to college because we would always have resources. Thoughts would race through my mind, and I felt blessed beyond reason.

Then came the day when Barry and I were finished. The way it ended was something I could never have foreseen or even imagined. It was so far removed from the man that I thought I knew. As it turns out, I didn't know him at all. The smooth operator and flashy lifestyle that made me fall for him were the very things that tore us apart.

Barry was a fraud!

CHAPTER 7

PROBATION AND CLUB TIBET

"Liberalism, above all, means emancipation—emancipation from one's fears, his inadequacies, from prejudice, from discrimination, from poverty."

~ Hubert H. Humphrey ~

I ENJOYED A LOT OF good times with Barry, my African prince while I still believed everything was real.

We hired a rental car while out in Florida on one of our lavish trips and I was driving back to the hotel to meet him with a few bottles of alcohol. Suddenly blue and red lights flickered behind me, and the threatening whoop of the police siren told me to pull over. I did.

In my mind I was just another citizen on the roads, trying to make my way back to the man I loved. Why were they bothering me? A burly, bearded police officer took one look at the alcohol on the front seat and asked me to get out of the car. "Why?" I asked, not sure of my rights. Could they treat me this way without cause?

"Miss, get out of the vehicle," the bearded officer repeated. He didn't have a friendly face. "Keep your hands where I can see them. Move slowly. We are going to search your vehicle."

"What do you mean search my car? What is this about? Why did you pull me over?"

My teenage mind had not grasped the concept of racial profiling just yet, and I refused to get out.

He yanked the door open and grabbed my arm to pull me out. Outraged, I yelled a profanity... a big mistake. He handcuffed me while the other policeman searched the car.

They found nothing, but this only made me protest even more. My big mouth! I should have held my tongue. They pushed me into the police car and took me back to the station, charged with obstruction of justice and driving without a driver's license. The charges were trumped up – it was my mouth and my color that had landed me in the cell. I'd forgotten my driver's license in a different hand-bag back at the hotel.

It was terrifying in that crowded holding cell, with its windowless walls, stained mattress and faint reek of vomit and urine. Unless I could raise bail money, I would get transferred to the women's annex prison with real criminals.

I contemplated calling my father, but discarded that idea.

"Why do you need bail money?" he would say. "You got yourself in there. I didn't send you! There is a place to sleep, food, and facilities. Your problem, it's like a hotel in there."

Or worse, he would help me, depleting his savings to take me out. I would forever feel guilty about that.

Luckily I had boyfriend to call.

Barry got it done—he sent the $2,000 bond release easily and set me free. I was so grateful.

The comforting feeling didn't last. About a week later, our relationship came to an emergency stop

It was a ordinary day. The sun was shining. I was in a great mood listening to some beats on the radio on the way to Barry's house. From a distance, those same red and blue lights flickered menacingly at me. The closer I got, the more my heart sank.

Police. On-lookers. Yellow police tape. What was going on?

I pulled into the driveway and found the house cordoned-off with tape. Stark black words on yellow plastic warned, *Crime Scene – Do Not Cross.*

I phoned Barry at once.

"Hello, girl." His voice sounded smooth and unconcerned.

"The police are at your house. What's going on here, Barry?" I asked him, my nerves on edge.

"Trust me, babe, nothing is going on. This is all a big misunderstanding. I was not involved here, but the police are looking for me. I can't get some of my stuff. Would you go inside and fetch a few things for me? Don't tell the police you have had any contact."

Of course I agreed. I picked my way through people into the house, explaining that I was Barry's girlfriend. This didn't have the impact I wanted. A policewoman sat me down and filled me in.

The house was ransacked. Everything was gone, there was nothing to collect. Worse yet, some kind of violent encounter had happened there.

The policewoman's eyes filled with dark concern. "Do you know where Barry is?"

I shook my head, in fright. Then the story came out.

The FBI was everywhere. People were taking photos of rooms, scrapes on the wall and collecting bits of evidence as I barely heard what the police woman was saying to me.

"Barry is a well-known drug dealer, a very dangerous man. Did you know that?"

I shook my head.

"He and his wife fled this morning, and the FBI is looking for him…"

Drugs. Dealing. Wife?

I couldn't grasp what she was saying. It was as if she was talking a foreign language I didn't understand.

The woman took my details and told me someone would come around to my house to question me later on in the week. With that news, I staggered off, in a non-reality of epic proportions.

Gradually, understanding trickled into my consciousness: Barry, the drug dealer. Barry, the married man. Barry, the liar.

Every moment I spent with him I had been 'the other woman.' Every second we shared together was a lie! Sure, we liked to party, but drug dealing? What had I gotten myself into?

Memories knocked and demanded admission. All of those times Barry left dinners to take secret phone calls, the way he spent money—it all made sense now.

As I closed the door of my car, tears flowed down my cheeks like Niagara Falls.

I had believed Barry to be my Black knight sent to save me from a life of boredom. Like an emotional vampire he fed off my youthful dreams and lust for excitement. I felt betrayed down to my core.

From that day, Barry vanished. He never came back, and I never went looking for him.

Barry taught me my first valuable lesson of love: men lie.

I resolved to be a lot more careful about whoever I fell for next time.

The aftermath of Barry's lies left me in a funk. I felt like Cinderella who, after dancing with the prince, had been cast back into a life of servitude, raking cinders.

At 21, I decided to get a more exciting job, and bluffed my way into a bartending position. How difficult could it be to pour drinks?

When a massive crowd pressed in at the bar, dozens of people at a time shouting for drinks I never even heard of, it dawned on me that confidence and charm might not be enough. I stared blankly at the woman shouting, "Get me a Shirley Temple, a side car and three mudslides."

To me, Shirley Temple was a fifties actress and mudslides were a natural disaster. My boss watched for an hour, then took me aside. "Crystal, that's the second time you have given a customer vodka and orange juice instead of what they asked for."

An hour into service and I was demoted to waitress, and I resolved to be the best waitress ever. I could hold a tray and look great writing orders on the little notepad. I could rock the ugly green apron. But I could barely get the orders at one table right, never mind five.

I hung onto the job just long enough to pass as a significantly below-average waitress, and to meet my second love, Tad. Everything about him was raw and real, so different from Barry.

Tad was outspoken and bold. He danced hard and partied harder. Once again, I found myself being courted by a tall, dark and handsome someone—only this time he was around my age—better, I thought. I spent months saving to buy my first car, a Honda Accord, with no help from my parents. Eventually I traded up to a 325i BMW.

Tad drove a BMW as well, and soon we were two BMW drivers in the throes of young love. My schedule became increasingly full as we dated, but we were both ambitious and wanted more out of life. Those were the planning years. I worked hard and dreamed of one day becoming a famous model or actress.

The more casting calls I went to, the more jobs I managed to book. My commercial auditions worked out well, and casting agents often chose me. I tried my best to juggle those auditions while temping as a waitress, but the commute from Long Island to the City, whether by Long Island railroad or on the Southern State Highway, left me exhausted.

I rode the highs, but Tad took up more and more of my time. I lost focus often, and instead of taking my modeling career seriously, I passed up opportunities.

Nobody told me what a fool I was. No one shook me by the shoulders and advised me to make something of myself while I could, and warned me that money wouldn't last forever.

My heart was never trained on an illustrious career; it was trained on the person I was in love with at the time. Tad was the man who captured my attention back then. We had a great time together. I came to love his frivolity and carefree nature.

CHAPTER 8

TAD THE DREAMER

"Save a boyfriend for a rainy day —
and another, in case it doesn't rain."

~ Mae West ~

TAD AND I FELL in love, but it was different. I kept a lot of my heart to myself this time. I was cautious about my feelings, even though the love I felt for him was real. He was exciting in a green way—daring and reckless. We would drive at top speed in his BMW just to enjoy the danger of it all.

Nothing was certain in Tad's life, and I liked that. With uncertainty comes a kind of freedom from the future, one where anything could happen. Maybe I would stay with Tad, maybe not. It didn't matter. We were young, and things were happening.

Then I was invited to participate in the Miss Jamaica American Beauty Pageant. As a model, I was used to the scene and I was always up for a new experience. Where modeling requires natural confidence, a pageant demands a ruthless attitude.

Those girls wanted to win, and they would step on your face to do it. I heard the craziest stories in the dressing rooms while preparing for the pageant stages. One girl broke the temperature control on another's flat iron and her hair burnt, leaving the room with a pungent, lingering odor. Another purposefully spilled a soft drink onto a competitor's evening gown. I stayed out of it. I had my beautiful, customized faux-Versace dress, some decent make-up, and a heartwarming speech prepared. Beyond that, I shut out the twittering and bickering of the other contestants.

Before the final stages of the competition that year, the girls expectantly banded together to complain about the 1 minute, 30 seconds speech time. "How are we supposed to show who we are in such a short amount of time?" they complained. I was relieved: without public speaking experience, a short speech suited me well.

The night of the competition was all about highs—high energy, high excitement, high heels and high platforms.

The backstage smelled of powders, foundations and antiperspirants. Nervous titters mingled with mumbled speech rehearsals and small squeals as girls panicked about a missing lipstick or loose stitches on the hem of their dress.

One of my sisters, Salome, arrived in the audience to give me support, holding a gigantic printed sign with my face on it! The evening was a blur of movement, queues and spotlights.

My modeling experience came in handy, and I struck the right poses at the right time. Then it was my turn for the speech. "I only want to make the world a better place, and I believe that is best achieved by changing one mind at a time."

The crowd loved me, though I couldn't fathom why. I left the stage to greet the horrified faces of the girls waiting off stage and to a thunderous applause that trailed behind me like smoke. All that remained was the judging now. If the girls belatedly saw me as a threat, they were too late to sabotage my eyelash tongs.

We all filed out on stage, a centipede of long, shining legs in clicking heels. "And now, for the crowning of your new Miss Jamaican American, please welcome…" Flashes of light littered the crowd as a tall, gorgeous woman glided onto the stage in a sparkly dress of blue sequins. She was holding a large, gem-encrusted crown.

Two other women joined her on stage with lesser crowns—the runners up. I remember breathing it all in—the energy from the crowd, the nerves of the women around me, the lights, the bustling world behind the curtains on stage. I didn't expect to win. I didn't expect to place anywhere. I had joined the pageant on a whim.

"Second princess…. Crystal!" the announcer said, and my name blossomed from his lips. I heard my name, but it was only when the girls on either side of me started to usher me down that I realized what had happened. Winning as second princess was a great, unexpected honor. They put a crown on my head and gave me the biggest bunch of flowers I ever held. Later on, I discovered that they also gave me the Photogenic Trophy. I was very humbled and fortunate.

My looks took me places like that, without any effort. I believed I was something special because my great looks brought me success.

That same evening, I met a young lawyer named Mr. Brockston, who was one of the pageant sponsors. Good thing too, because he saved me more than once from the law and the stupidity of youthful impulses. Being a model was great, but it didn't pay well unless you were a supermodel. After I won a crown at the pageant, the pressure got that much worse.

I needed to be stunningly gorgeous, all the time, and that included wearing the latest designer gear which I couldn't afford on the earnings from my modeling and temp job.

Good thing I knew ways to get clothes by methods other than paying the full price. But before long, this landed me in trouble.

The shop's security guards stopped my friend and searched our bag, revealing three designer tops and a pair of gold earrings—damning evidence. My good looks didn't help, and my charm was wasted on those men.

Luckily my pageant attorney friend Mr. Brockston arrived at the police station to sort things out. He even represented us in court and got us off on a light sentence.

I got three years' probation as a first offender, and a $300 fine. At the time I was thoroughly outraged, but things could have been a lot worse. I could have gone to jail. It would have ruined my entire life—for what? Three average tops and fake gold earrings.

That was a wake-up call for me.

I decided to kick the boosting habit. Aside from the embarrassment of being caught, I had risked my freedom and my future—two things I couldn't afford to lose.

Now I had to juggle my modeling and temp work with probation meetings, like a circus clown trying to keep many balls in the air at once.

For all of my posturing and good looks, my crown and my natural feistiness, it could all go away in the blink of an eye. For the second and final time, I had been on the wrong side of the law.

"Three strikes and you're out!" my mom shouted at me the next time I saw her.

Those words were not lost on me. I had to grow up, and fast. The days of being a teenager were gone, and while I was still blooming into my looks—my childhood was already in the rear-view mirror. I let go of my old beliefs that I could walk the line between success and being 'a little bit of a criminal.'

Tad was supportive, but his career was taking on new dimensions and we were seeing each other less. He was growing up too, which meant longer hours. Of course, I didn't like it. I still wanted to party and be the center of attention at the club.

Fresh from a year of starring in famous brand advertisements and winning a crown in a big time beauty pageant, I was a minor celebrity in a city full of nobodies. It was an amazing feeling, and the attention that surrounded me was equally as amazing. At times, I thought my head was going to fly off from the rush of it all.

New York City was my play thing, and I was open once again to new experiences. "Don't let it go to your head," Tad warned me, but what did he know? He wasn't in the middle of the storm. He wasn't on the rise, like I was.

"Why do you always have to ruin my fun, man?" I complained whenever he refused to meet me at the club. "You are going to have to work harder to make me happy."

What a head I had! Tad and I stayed together for three years. It was a fundamental three years that impacted my life in a lot of ways.

My modeling career was taking off, and I had more friends than I could count. At the same time, people seemed to gravitate towards me like I was a magnet. I was proud to be the most fun, the most attractive, and the most wild-spirited person they knew.

"Where do you think you are going to be in five years, Crystal?" friends sometimes asked me.

"Not sure. It depends what offers and opportunities come my way. I might go into acting, but I'm enjoying modeling right now, too."

"You must have a plan though."

"My plan is to keep having fun, for as long as I can," I would joke.

Only, it was not a joke. I meant it. I wanted those days to last. As Tad settled into his regular job, working like a hamster on a spinning wheel—I saw great opportunities around me and didn't hesitate to go with it. Fun was something I should have had a master's degree in.

I tasted fame now, directly from the cup. I never wanted to let it go. That was what caused me to distance myself from Tad. We were moving in different directions now for quite some time. He was ready to work hard and settle down.

I was ready to play hard and rise up, however I could, and Tad now felt like an anchor holding me back. He would always treat me like the struggling waitress he met at Club Tibet. I didn't want to be that person anymore. I wanted more. I wanted it all.

With my ever-growing ego and a popularity that rivaled celebrity status—the next best thing to come along was another love. I didn't know it yet, but that person would become a central part of my life for the rest of my life. Poor Tad, he never stood a chance.

CHAPTER 9

MAX THE HIGH FLYER

"If you love someone, set them free. If they come back they're yours; if they don't they never were."

~ Richard Bach ~

MAX STEPPED INTO MY life at the right time. I was on a return trip from Kingston, Jamaica—walking to my car at Kennedy Airport in New York City when I noticed him for the first time. A chance encounter, but one that would change my life forever.

I was traveling with the designers of Nearly Yardy. We exited the terminal in force, and I split from them to find my mom who was waiting for me outside the parking area. Airport traffic always confused my mom, so to make it easier for her I would walk the extra distance to a meeting place she could manage.

This time, it turned out that destiny had a hand in the experience. I felt his eyes on me the moment I stopped at my mother's car. "Crystal, lovely to see you again—how was your trip?" my mother began, as my attention became split between her greeting and the feeling that I was being watched.

I looked behind me, and there he was. A well-dressed man in a black Lexus, wearing what I thought looked like a hat from the movie Crocodile

Dundee! I was instantly intrigued by his gaze. Then he left. "Who was that?" Mom asked, but I didn't know. I continued loading my bags into the boot of her blue sedan.

Suddenly, a car pulled up across the road—that same Lexus. He was back! What on earth was he doing? The car horn beeped as I bent over to push my bag deeper into the boot. Enough was enough.

I shut the boot and marched across the road to the car. "What are you hooting at me for?"

"I…I…um…" He took a breath. "Couldn't help it girl, those jeans!"

I smiled at him. He seemed sweet, but Mom was growing impatient and he was not making a move. "If you like what you see, why don't you ask for my number already and we can get to know each other?" I pushed.

It was that simple. He took my number and called me the same night. I should have listened to my mother when she said that he looked like a womanizer.

Young and reckless, I already resigned myself to the fact that Tad and I were fading. He didn't have what I wanted. With one relationship dying, another struck up quickly with Max, the man from the airport parking lot.

I had no idea that Tad was keeping an eye on me. He somehow discovered the code to my answering machine, and when I started messing around with Max—he knew about it.

One night, as we were watching a movie, Tad confronted me. "Who is this man you are always seeing, Crystal?" he demanded. "I know there is someone else. Come clean now. You can't have both of us; you have to choose."

He made a compelling case, and we had a lot of history together. I reassured him and that same evening we wandered out into the City and got matching tattoos of each other's names.

Good thing Max had no idea what a 'Tad' was, so the name was easy enough to disguise as something else.

I didn't know what I wanted and I thought I could have it all. Everyone wanted a piece of me, and I was determined not to let those experiences go to waste.

I clicked along with Tad for some time after the tattoos, but eventually he got the message that our relationship was finished.

Max was a juggernaut, a big shot, in ways I hardly understood at the time. An intellectual, down to earth kind of guy—he was everything I was looking for. It was a year in when everything fell apart for Tad. I had no real understanding of just how well-known Max was, or the level of his importance at the bank where he worked.

Max not only had wealth, he acquired power—real power, the kind that sent people scurrying around to make him happy. I was hooked, and when the day came I needed to tell Tad we were over. Tad arrived at my house, wanting to speak to me again about Max.

In my driveway was a brand new Mercedes Benz that Max gifted to me the night before. I left the house and met him outside by the car. I could see on his face; he knew it was over.

"That man bought you this?" he asked me, crestfallen. He was defeated. Tad couldn't give me the kind of lifestyle I wanted, and he knew it.

I nodded and told him it was best if we broke it off. He took it graciously, although I realized later how much my betrayal must have hurt him, and how lightly I had played with his heart.

And so, my relationship with Tad fizzled out. He taught me that even though good intentions can fill you with joy, without money they don't mean anything. Money made the world go around.

I had been invited into the world of high end luxury, and that kind of lifestyle blinds a girl. Wolford and Laperla, Manolos Blahniks, Chanel and Fendi furs—these were things Max gifted me. I added 'rich' to my list of must-haves in men.

All I needed in the world was an honest, wealthy man who loved me. Max was that man. He told me repeatedly that he would prove that to me forever, if that is what it took.

Once Tad was out of the picture, I fell deeper in love with Max. His wealth and power amplified everything he did. Even his small gestures were huge, and it was easy to get caught up in that lavish lifestyle all over again. Max was an honest man with a real career that gave him his wealth. He was Barry and Tad rolled into one.

Dating Max was an adventure for my young heart. He would pick me up in a limo with a gigantic bunch of exotic flowers whenever we went out, wearing his sexy salmon colored sports jacket. The same height as me, Max was a very attractive man with fine features.

It was not long after leaving Tad that things got serious for Max and me. It was a heady romance that boomed into our lives. We wanted to spend all of our free time together, having fun and living life. Was this my paradise? I believed it was.

Max regularly surprised me with gifts: a membership at an exclusive sports center at Chelsea Piers, jewelry I was sometimes afraid to wear because it was worth so much, and dinners that could have paid several middle class mortgages. Then, the gift that blew my mind. He led me down the hall of a prominent building in the City, and opened the door to a brand new apartment, just for me. My dreams were coming true, and it was all thanks to Max loving me and his generosity.

Still, a worry niggled at the back of my mind. So much wealth, surely if a man like this wanted to—he could have other women all over the City. Would I ever find out? Was Max as honest as he claimed to be? Doubts started trickling in, but I pushed them aside.

Max had organized to have the apartment customized and decorated to my tastes. We quickly became fierce lovers as well as best friends, and I felt closer to him than I ever had felt with any other man.

Beyond the generosity, and the fact that he helped pay for my degree in Applied Science with a Minor in Advertising and BS in Marketing Communications—he also sat with me each night helping me get through my math course, quantitative statistics. He put in the time, the love, his presence. I had it all.

For several months, Max courted me in extreme style. He took me on vacations that would have impressed Barry, and I soon realized that he was in a whole different league to the wealth I had believed my African prince held.

Max was an extremely ambitious man, and he worked constantly. With a golden tongue and a relaxed aura, he closed business deals like there was no tomorrow. But Max had his problems too—he loved to party and that came with a certain amount of drama, especially when alcohol and other substances were involved.

Still, I couldn't have been happier. He plucked me from my boring, limited life as a somewhat successful model and beauty pageant winner and gave me something better. When I was with Max, I acquired power too.

The closer we became, the more it felt like his success was my success. I devoted myself to keeping him happy. I ditched work and started to shape my days around what he needed. I gave it all to him, because he deserved it.

Max swept me off my feet. I owned a luxury apartment, a brand new car, a closet-full of outrageously expensive clothing and jewelry, and the ability to do whatever I wanted. For me, this was the closest to heaven I had ever been.

I didn't think about the cost but opened my arms and embraced the good fortune.

The two of us were jetsetters, and the world was our playground. Max loved my feisty attitude, and how I never let people get in my way. I commanded respect, even when I didn't have any money. That was why he fell in love with me.

My new true love soon eclipsed the memory of Tad.

CHAPTER 10

WEDDING BELLS

"There's a big difference between falling in love with someone and falling in love with someone and getting married. Usually, after you get married, you fall in love with the person even more."

~ Dave Grohl ~

AFTER A WILD NIGHT out I proposed marriage. Max couldn't have been happier. Soon after, the date was set and we were engaged to be married.

Our initial wedding plans fell through—Max was going through something heavy at work and was partying a lot. Alcohol was flowing like an endless river, the best and most expensive, of course.

We got back on course and made new plans. The night before the wedding Max surprised me with a trip to Atlantic City for the pre-party with tickets to see Whitney Houston perform, a long-time favorite of mine. A big group of us dressed in our furs and finery, ant got into a limo to Atlantic City.

The ride alone was a massive party, once we arrived there—it was a one stop candy shop of lavish experiences. I met up with an old model friend of mine who was one of Whitney's dancers, and we all partied together until the morning of my wedding.

It was an extravagant wedding, I showed up an hour late to the church ceremony in Brooklyn, still trying to shake off the revelry of the night before. Max always did that far better than I did.

After an exquisite reception with more than 150 guests in a Manhattan club, we continued partying in a nightclub.

Our groomsmen partied even harder than the previous night, drinking everything in sight—the more expensive, the better. Max and I were so drunk we nearly forgot to cut the cake The amazing band, a DJ and a wedding singer rocked the place. Boy, did we enjoy ourselves!

Max was in such high spirits that he leaped onto the table to dance, but the table leg broke and collapsed. Smoothly and effortlessly, he landed neatly on the floor beside the ruined table—nothing could bring him down from his revelry.

I was blessed with five beautiful bridesmaids, and my mom, the matron of honor. Makeup extraordinaire Chanel did my face and Al Allure my hair, costing a grip, but the time for scrimping was in the past. My colors were white and green, fresh and bright. Everything was wonderful.

But drama was brewing. Around the time of my wedding to Max, I discovered spite and envy in the people closest to me. False friends simmered with resentment that I had made such a good catch. They wanted a shot at my husband and lifestyle.

I chose to be positive about my marriage to Max, but I needed to be on guard all the time, and it was ridiculous.

When I was younger, I had dreamed of getting into broadcasting or a different career in fashion, but those ideas fell aside when I got married and became a willing slave to my husband's every whim.

Soon after we were married, a trip was booked on the Concord for the first time. The infamous Concord Airline to Paris, France from JFK to be exact. It crunched a standard eight-hour flight into a four-hour luxury party cruise on a private airline.

With no idea what to expect as we boarded, I was confronted with opulence and airline luxury that I never experienced before. At $10,000 a ticket, this high-end flight was so top notch you cannot even go on them anymore.

A bottle of champagne was an awaiting accommodation on our flight. It came from some rare vineyard somewhere in France, where we were heading. The cutlery was made of solid silver—even the seats in the plane were made from the softest, best leather.

Restaurant quality food, expensive alcohol, and an extravagant place to nap if you felt like it… were all part of the experience. We were waited on hand and foot by the staff on board. I felt like a queen, and Max was my king. Husband and wife—together forever.

Max was a man on a mission. Wherever we went, whoever we were with—these were the elite of the world. I met celebrities and influential people, shook hands with Michelle and Barack Obama, hobnobbed with the best in the finance, music and business industries. No one was out of reach.

I clung to the idea that I was enough for him, but Max was a man of many great appetites. And always I lived with the fear that one day things would change.

Max and I eventually became pregnant with twins. It was a turning point in Max's life—he was to become a father for the first time and realized it was time to slow the partying down, so that we could settle and grow as a family.

The only problem was that Max was terrible at it. Soon a time came for me and my very pregnant belly to perform. I was driving somewhere when my water suddenly broke.

I just managed to get myself to the nearest hospital. It was not my first choice of establishment, and I didn't want to have the twins in this shabby environment. But they were coming and after the doctor saw me, I was immediately booked in for an emergency C section.

Things happened fast after that. I remember wanting Max to be there, but the staff couldn't get hold of him. Despite the neglected building and facilities, the staff members were clued up and professional.

At 3am I gave birth to twins, a beautiful boy and girl. The experience was headier than the finest champagne or the most lavish experience, more emotional than anything I felt before.

Here were these cute little babies, right in my arms. Max rushed to my side after the birth, when they finally got hold of him. He was the proudest father. That was when we knew that for better or worse, our lives were now tied together by the twins.

Having newborn babies was a life-changing experience for me. I wouldn't have traded all the fancy cars and Concord rides in the world, for a single moment with my babies. They were the center of my universe and a new reason to build a happy life with their father.

Max was enamored by the arrival of our babies. The twins didn't want for anything. They had the best care, the finest clothes and enough toys to load into a truck and donate to a small village of children far away.

For a time, we were genuinely happy, but eventually the late nights and ongoing demands irked Max. He was a fast-paced, important man with more experience drinking and partying than being a loving, attentive father. He left the parenting to me and continued enjoying himself. I was happy to stay with the twins, who needed me.

Max was an amazing provider. Throughout my time raising the twins in those first years, we never went without anything we wanted, needed or thought about. At a moment's notice, Max would take us to an island somewhere for a brief holiday—if things got too hectic.

The twins thrived and learned quickly. I watched as they advanced faster than other children I knew because they were fortunate to have the best of everything. I watched and thought of my own childhood, and how lean it had been for us. Indeed, I was living a blessed life.

But Max had to go away on trips without me more frequently. I saw it happening, but thought it was for the best. This is how another woman started making her way into our lives—the secret mistress who entertained my husband in my absence.

CHAPTER 11

THE CONCORD LIFE

"You can never control who you fall in love with, even when you're in the most sad, confused time of your life. You don't fall in love with people because they're fun. It just happens."

~ Kirsten Dunst ~

WITH MAX, EVERY DAY was pure excitement. I was living the affluent life, fresh from a dream that I somehow stepped into. When the twins were a little older, we left them with a professional child care expert and Max took me to St. Barth for the biggest celebrity wedding celebration.

I arrived at the St. Barth docks to find an array of elites wandering on and off a huge yacht, the size of several large apartments. From the outside it looked as though the yacht itself could comfortably sleep fifty or more people. I had never seen anything so opulent!

Better yet, the entire yacht was adorned in whites and beach colors, with multiple decks where you could sit and chat with friends, and many indoor bar areas that were loaded with canapés, snacks and expensive bottles of champagne and wine.

For the first time in a long time, I felt a little out of my depth. Luckily my sassy attitude was always an asset for me in those situations. Celebrity faces were all over the yacht, and no expense was spared for the wedding that would take place there.

Max knew Michael Jordan well, and Jordan apparently wanted to make a statement with the events and luxury of the day. With such status, there were a lot of secrets floating around. Husbands were only faithful to their wives in concept. Meanwhile, behind closed doors almost anyone was up for grabs.

More than once, as Max was engaged in conversation with industry types, I milled around finding my own fun. I was pulled into a beautiful blue room by one charming man, who wanted to get intimate. And it happened again when I was exploring the top deck, sitting under a copse of umbrellas by the main bar. As a good wife, I excused myself from these situations to maintain my husband's integrity.

While on the top deck, sipping colorful cocktails and reclining with several interesting people around me, I looked down to find Max engrossed in conversation with a young woman. I could instantly tell that his interest went beyond the quality of her words.

I decided it was a fair time to head back down to him, in case he was tempted by a quick cabin hook-up. I moved quickly and interrupted their conversation. "This is my wife, Crystal…" he said to the woman. She left soon after that.

"What are you doing talking to that lame chick?" I asked him frankly. Subtlety was never my strong point.

"Come on, honey, I was just making conversation. She works in finance. Do you have to be jealous of everyone I speak to?" The faint irritation in his voice told me I had inconvenienced him, or ended a game that he had been playing with her.

"I get to be jealous of anyone that you flirt so openly with," I reminded him from behind my Chanel sunglasses.

He quietly shook his head and sipped on his champagne. "It's the same every time with you, isn't it?" he said into the distance.

"Don't try and make this about me, Max. You were the one touching her arm and turning on the charm."

It was not the first time I'd caught Max flirted so obviously with another woman. He'd already been unfaithful once, and I'd been watching him closely ever since.

I regularly fought with Max about his predilection for other women. I was convinced that he was playing me, and he insisted he wasn't. Many of the fights ended in one of us leaving, or a lingering grumpiness that grew more and more sour as our relationship wore on.

Max was a good man, but he was also good-looking, smart and libidinous. He loved partying, and women were a natural by-product of that lust. Then the day came when his dirty laundry was aired.

The year we were getting married I found texts between him and another woman named Gina, a light-skinned black with pronounced cheekbones. It was clear that they were having some kind of affair.

I forced him to call her in front of me and break it off. "I'm getting married next week," he said, "and I don't want to drag this into my marriage. It's over."

I was satisfied. He swore that it would end when we got married, and I believed that it did. Max did an outstanding job keeping his affair with Gina a secret from me.

Then, the day came when it all unraveled for him, and I was there to watch it happen. Max took me on a trip to Europe—I complained because he had been going there a lot lately, and staying for one or two weeks at a time, every time. He took me to France, and we stayed in a palatial hotel right in the center of Paris.

All of a sudden I was called back to the States on some work emergency, three days into the holiday. "You head back home I still have business to do here," Max told me. He didn't know I had found a hotel confirmation booking that he had made down the street. Instead of leaving, I waited for him in the lobby of that hotel.

Eventually, in he wheeled with all of his luggage and someone else's too—a woman's! I stood in the middle of the hallway, blocking his progress.

He looked first, utterly confused, then sheepish and ashamed.

"Surprised to see me here, Max? One would think that you would be glad to see your wife didn't have to hurry away to another country on our holiday. But you're not here on business are you? You're here with Gina."

I could see on his rat lying face that I was right.

To avoid a hotel lobby scene, I followed him up to their room. Everything was rather silent. We spoke briefly and he decided to cancel the booking and come home with me. We left for the airport, and he brought Gina's stuff with him.

"And all of this cheap rubbish?" I gestured at Gina's luggage with disdain. Actually, some of the items were nice.

"You can have it," Max said, still in a mess of trouble.

"I don't want it. But I'm sure my friends will have a great time sharing out her trashy clothing choices," I said sharply.

We hopped on the earliest Concord and headed back home. Nothing was ever the same after that. I could no longer trust anything my husband said to me. Inevitably, this led to more fighting and mistrust. I was suspicious of his every move.

There are some things a marriage cannot get over. A long-term affair with another woman is one of them. Back when I believed that Max was just hooking up with her before our marriage, sure—I could find forgiveness in my heart. But now she may as well have declared war on me.

I filed for a divorce, and we ended our union shortly after that. Once again, I was left with almost nothing. Max provided generous support for his children—but beyond that I had to make my own way in the world again.

I bought a condo in Long Island City and moved in with the twins.

Divorcing Max turned out to be a wise move. I was returning home from a business trip—and there was Max's face on CNN. He got arrested along with his partner on money-laundering charges.

It was a massive blow to Max and a big deal for our family. After the market turn-down, Max had allegedly become involved in some shady dealings. Federal agent arms deals and money-laundering are not small charges. I could hardly believe it, but then again—I knew nothing about the things Max did.

Max was caught trying to flee the country on a yacht. The FBI moved in and arrested him. Max went to prison and lost his money, his properties, and his lifestyle.

It was the right decision to leave Max. Still—in my heart, the pain of betrayal grew. Were there no good men left in the world? Did all men cheat?

Ah, Max. He was so wild and carefree. Pity he wasn't a little more careful when it came to his decisions.

Being with Max taught me a lot of important lessons; above all, that wealth, as wonderful as it was, meant nothing if the person you loved didn't share their entire life with you.

I added a new lesson to my growing life lesson on men. Money was important—but the person behind the money needed to know how to spend it wisely and manage it correctly. He also had to be honest and treat me with respect.

The next man that I became interested in would have to have all of these boxes checked before I became involved. I was still beautiful and could rebuild my life.

CHAPTER 12

ALONE AGAIN?

"Loneliness is my least favorite thing about life. The thing that I'm most worried about is just being alone without anybody to care for or someone who will care for me."

~ Anne Hathaway ~

HAVING TO LEAVE MAX was yet another major lifestyle adjustment, and I decided to take the opportunity to enter the field of broadcasting.

Using my connections, I got a radio broadcasting apprenticeship program. Theoretically, I was primed for success. Realistically, there were few openings and just not enough money in radio when you have no real following. Broadcasting turned out to be a savage business that left me feeling vulnerable and helpless.

With twins to look after, and an ex-husband facing serious charges and time in prison, I needed stability, fast.

Over the years, rubbing shoulders with high society taught me a thing or two. I had developed skills. They may not have been the kind of skills that automatically make a person rich, but I could definitely use them in another field.

When an opening arose with a big financial company, I jumped at the chance. It was decent pay and the people there were motivated to succeed. I targeted wealthy clients, and connected with them because of my past life as one of the super-rich. It was the most direct path to success for me. I did well in this challenging career because I had a natural knack for selling to top tier clients.

The twins were adjusting to life without their father. They still saw each other as often as time would allow, but Max had a lot on his plate. The biggest thing for Max, I think, was realizing that he couldn't just have whatever he wanted any more.

For the first time in my life I felt responsible for my own family unit. I had twins, and I was alone. I had my own job, and my own apartment. I was bringing in decent amounts of money, even if I couldn't afford what I once could.

These were some of the hardest, yet some of the most invigorating days of my life. I relearned the price of things, and began to value what I had twice as much.

I swore off men for a while. My heart suffered considerably after Max, and I was hyper-suspicious of any man who took interest in me purely because of my looks. I didn't want to end up with another cheater, though a part of me also accepted that most men would cheat if they could.

My girlfriends and I came to the conclusion that love relationships were almost pointless, and much harder to sustain in an unequal marriage, or where the man has all of the power. With unlimited resources come endless curiosity, we would say. Most men couldn't control themselves.

I had spent enough time rebuffing advances from other men at those parties. I could only begin to imagine how much more aggressive some women would be with a powerful man. It made me melancholy and a little ill inside to think about it.

I promised myself that I wouldn't let the twins grow up to be players, crushing hearts—and that was that. I let it go. I focused on my work and doing well for my family. I took on more and more clients, and earned commission to match.

I forgot about men and partying, and living like a member of the super-rich. Things were normal, peaceful. Then after a few years, another man stepped into my life. It took me by surprise, just as much as it took him by surprise. My days of romance were far from over.

CJ was referred to me by a friend, as a client who was looking for a financial advisor. He was tall, far taller than any man I had been with and in control, he knew what he wanted. When I first met him, he told me that he graduated from Wharton Business School and that he worked at Merrill Lynch.

There was something dark and brooding about CJ that attracted me to him. Plus, he was comfortably well-off, allowing a lifestyle of relative luxury.

The first time CJ asked me on a date, I declined — but we kept meeting for financial management discussions and things progressed from there. He was blessed with a deep magnetic pull, something that was very desirable for me at the time.

It was something of a whirlwind romance. He kept asking, and eventually I lost the will to refuse him. To a single mother of a two, a man in charge was an attraction. Of course, I had no idea how in charge CJ liked to be.

When we were at restaurants, he ordered for me. When we were shopping, he picked out my clothes. He was possessive in a way that I had never experienced before. The love was intense and overwhelming—finally a man who wanted to spend all of his time with me!

CJ and I spent entire weekends together, shutting out the world and delighting in the passion we found together. Once again, I was flying on cloud nine. He did everything right. CJ was the perfect gentleman, and he showed me off to his friends and family like I was the most amazing jewel in the room.

Every now and then in those early days he got jealous, too. Even though he was dashing and handsome, he always lingered when I spoke to other men and complained heavily about it afterwards.

"It's just cause I love you, babe," he explained. I liked that, because I wanted to be the center of his entire world. I believed that CJ was the man I'd been searching for.

In many ways, CJ was the opposite of Max. He was always in control and knew what was happening with his money. He was very demanding and knew what he wanted from life. He was proud to be a strait-laced, honest man.

On paper, CJ was one of the best things at that time that happened to me. We flew to Nice, France for the weekend and he proposed with a five-carat flawless diamond ring. It was a moment filled with ecstasy, and I gladly accepted his proposal—my heart full of love and joy again.

After the engagement, we moved in together, and that was when things started to go awry. The apartment in the Metropolis Building in Long Island City that we bought together had both of our names on the deed. I really had to fight for it, but I insisted and he gave in.

Living with CJ became a considerable nightmare. It was like a switch had been flipped the moment I agreed to marry him. Suddenly his money was more important than mine. He insisted on taking ownership of things that belonged to me. His natural air of leadership dissolved into control-seeking behaviors.

CJ and I went to trade in my car, and he paid in a little extra so that I could get a Porsche, a car I always wanted. Because of that, he demanded that his name go in the contract as co-owner. At first, I was confused by it but deep down I knew it was wrong. Was CJ trying to control me by taking control of everything I owned?

I heard about men like this from my friends. Before CJ, all the men I dated were generous people. They let me live my life, and I let them live theirs. But CJ was different. He had been growing considerably more jealous and controlling since we moved in together. He said things like, "Are you going to wear that out? What message does it send?" and "You're not hanging out with her again, are you? I don't like her."

Within three months of living with CJ, I realized what a mistake I made. I had agreed to marry a control freak who wouldn't be happy until I was doing everything he told me to do. We fought constantly, because I was not the kind of woman to submit to a man's will.

One evening we had a particularly bad fight, and I told him I didn't want to marry him anymore. He grabbed my hand and pulled off my engagement ring. Then he stormed out of the apartment, like I set him on fire.

I immediately messaged him and apologized, because I felt so guilty. He made me feel like saying those words was the same as stabbing him in the back. No one could make me feel guilt like CJ could.

But that was what it was like being with CJ. If you hurt him, he hurt you back twice as badly. We made up and I got my ring back, but I sensed that marrying CJ would be a fundamental mistake of epic proportions.

Then, on a photo shoot that I booked in Bermuda, I took my engagement ring off and lost it at Elbow Beach. I searched all day and got every staff member involved, but I couldn't find it. I suspected someone had stolen it.

Worse yet was the fear that was setting in my heart. How was I going to explain to CJ that I lost my engagement ring? He wouldn't believe me. He would accuse me of cheating on him. He would go crazy that I lost his precious, expensive ring.

There was no choice but to return home and face the music with CJ. I explained what had happened and waited for the blow out.

"That's fine, honey, you are insured right?" he asked me.

"Yeah, I am."

"Okay then. Claim from insurance and give me the cash back. You've already had your ring and you've lost it. Now I want my money returned."

"What do you mean? Are you punishing me for losing the ring?"

He smiled at me. "It's clear you can't look after something so valuable, so we will get you something smaller. It will be much better for you."

I had a big problem with CJ and I knew it. From that point I was like a magnet for his abusive comments. I would have to break it off. Still raw from my recent divorce, and now tied into financial constraints with CJ, I felt like I had stepped into a Vietnamese bamboo trap.

CHAPTER 13

BURT ARRIVES

"Once you learn to be happy, you won't tolerate being around
people who make you feel anything less."

~ Germany Kent ~

WHY DID I FALL for every man that I was attracted to? I sat up on the king size bed in my New York apartment, looking out over the city—remembering those feelings of helplessness with CJ. Then I still managed to get involved with Burt after that. And now this. Again! I was an idiot.

The bed felt cold under my body and the room was silent. The nanny was doing her job with James in the other room. I wanted to disappear. Somehow, my choice in men was strange. I felt a volcano of emotions waiting to erupt inside me.

Part of me wanted to set my closet on fire; another part didn't want to let it go. 'This is what happens when you live inside a man's life', I told myself. I thought I had learned my lessons. But life never stopped teaching me new lessons.

I leaned over and picked up the phone, which was on Burt's side of the bed. It rang once, twice…three times. My father answered, "Hello?"

"Hi Dad. Listen, could I come stay with you two for a few days?" I asked tentatively.

"Ah, child, what happened?"

"Burt is cheating on me. I need time to think about things and find somewhere to live."

"Well, you are always welcome here, Crystal. You pack your stuff and I'll send your mother over with the car to help you."

I hung up, feeling raw and tingly. A mild heat was building up all around me, turning my skin cold. I was walking through the gauntlet again.

I truly believed that Burt was the man I had waited for my entire life. He seemed honest, at least in his business dealings—a good and attentive father, a kind and generous man to me. He had Tad's carefree spirit and Barry and Max's ambition. There was even an intensity about him that I enjoyed in CJ.

I had given up my steady career being a financial advisor to be with him. Was I fated to make the same mistakes over and over, doomed to throw my life away for love every time?

I bustled into the adjoining room where my enormous digital closet was housed.

It was glorious. And now I would probably have to build a new life again. I pulled out the bags the maid had just finished unpacking from our Cabo trip, and threw this and that into it. I packed with a kind of sour determination.

At that moment, I hated men. All of them! When I thought of the relationships that had ended because of another woman, my stomach fermented with sour resentment. I threw top after top into my bag, unable to choose what to take with me. I was caught in a hail of designer wear.

Eventually, I collapsed onto my couch, tears streaming down my face once more. I would move out. I didn't have choice. I wouldn't be a man's plaything, a toy to be used when his other toys were not available. I was worthy of respect and dignity. I deserved a good and honest man.

The nanny poked her head into the closet room. "Are you okay, Ms.?"

I quickly wiped the tears from my eyes.

"I'm okay, thank you. Just make sure that James is happy. We may have to pack some of his things. We're leaving this house… tonight."

She nodded and returned to my son, who was messing around with some of his Star Wars Legos.

That was the worst of it. I would have to rip James away from his father, and all because he couldn't behave himself. The twins and James would have to live with me in whatever home I could make for them. That was life.

I would never consider staying. More damage could be done to kids when they see their mother allowing their father to treat them badly. I wouldn't let my kids grow up to be as careless with their hearts. They would learn to treat women well.

At the time I met Burt, CJ and I were barely holding our relationship together. With every controlling slur, he pushed me away.

I met a charming gentleman who was referred to me by a friend for a financial advisor meeting.

I usually dislike it when my clients bring along other people. Those tend to waste time and ask questions that have nothing to do with the plan I am trying to sell. But the gentleman brought along his key man, Burt.

That first meeting I could tell from Burt's body language and general vibe that he found me attractive. He staged a little fight with his fiancée, and then told me how their engagement was coming to an end. We bonded over our relationships that were both ending.

That glorious day, he signed and locked me down as his financial advisor. Soon after that Burt started visiting me at my office, for all sorts of reasons — he needed me to look at a clause in his policy or he wanted to meet me for lunch to discuss expanding his benefits.

I told him very clearly at first that I was in no position to date. I was still engaged, and I had to figure out how to end it peacefully, without drama. Burt took that as a challenge, and suddenly we were on a double date together.

CJ didn't like Burt one bit; I think he could feel the vibes between us. I can't say that Burt's fiancée liked me either; she could also feel the sexual energy flying back and forth over the table. By the end of the night, she stormed off in a huff.

While CJ was in the bathroom, Burt hugged me goodbye. I inhaled his scent – clean and fresh as if he had just stepped out of the shower with a luxurious woody aftershave. That was when I knew I wanted him. I melted into his arms.

By the time I arrived home with CJ and he started his usual jealous tirades, I had already decided that I would have a fling with Burt.

The next day Burt messaged me. We started going to long lunches together, and this progressed to nights out on the town. I would tell CJ that I needed to attend business meetings or chill with friends.

I made more and more excuses to CJ so that I could be with Burt who came with me to parties. Suddenly I was being wooed by my kind of man all over again. I had not realized it at the time, but Burt was major league. Best of all, he was a dream lover. Everything about him aroused me, from his soft touch to his way with people. He demanded respect, but he treated people well. He was generous, but never to an extreme excess. He was suave, smart, and full of life.

My heart was already limping around from the disaster of my previous marriage and my impending break-up with CJ. Burt was my White knight in shining armor, come to save me from the mistakes of my past.

Every time I went out with Burt, I came home to CJ. He looked at me with increasing suspicion, which didn't do anything but irritate me.

Between going to parties with Burt and being controlled by CJ, I was in a kind of catch-22 situation. Out of respect for the passion that we had once shared, I hung in there. I wanted to see if CJ could stop his controlling nature and return to the man I had fallen for some months before that. I guess what I was doing didn't help the situation, but it was his own fault.

Burt would spend long hours talking to me about breaking it off with CJ. He took the first step and broke it off with his fiancée, but made it clear it wasn't because of me. I appreciated that.

For a while I had been worried that if he could cheat on her, he could eventually cheat on me. All I knew was that Burt wanted me, and he would do anything to have me. I needed to feel that way.

Now I wondered if he had pursued Layaho, or whoever his new mistress was, with the same energy and enthusiasm he had once applied to courting me. Did they start meeting for long lunches? He already admitted that they reached that stage.

Had he hugged her in the same way he hugged me? My insides turned cold. All of those nights when Burt said he had to work late. Is anything real in this world? Does love ever last? A broken heart is a heavy thing to carry around with you. Disastrously…Heavy!

I justified my actions to myself: I was doing this because CJ was so cruel to me. I was afraid of what he would do if I wanted to leave him. Would he try and take my car and the apartment? Everything had been so uncertain then—everything but my blossoming love for Burt. That bastard!

I was tempted to throw all of his clothes out of the window, just to get the satisfaction of seeing them flutter to the ground below. Then I tucked those wild thoughts away. I wouldn't want to cause an accident in the street.

Burt might be a player, but I had done my fair share of playing as well. Perhaps this was the universe telling me that the right man was yet to come into my life.

CHAPTER 14

BURT FINDS A WAY

*"All good is hard. All evil is easy. Dying, losing, cheating, and
mediocrity is easy. Stay away from easy."*

~ Scott Alexander ~

THE ROMANCE BETWEEN BURT and me grew each time I saw him.
I often sneaked away during the day to meet him at a local café
for coffee, and we planned events together that CJ would know
nothing about.

It was treacherous, dangerous, and exciting. I was doing something
I had never done before, and in some small way I felt vindicated.

CJ was becoming increasingly hostile towards me, and I didn't like
it. It led me to Burt, and a much fuller, more genuine relationship than I
had experienced with CJ.

CJ was a very physical man; he was intense and bold, but he was not
considerate, a serious drawback in his personality. It got to the point where
I felt like each of his commands was a slight against me. He never did
replace my engagement ring, instead he chose to keep the money. That was
a choice he made—to give me a gift and then take it away. I couldn't take
a man like that seriously, not when his attentions were so easy to repeal.

I left CJ in my heart a while before the truth about Burt and me was revealed. I could tell that Burt was in it for the right reasons, and for marriage too. The closer I got to him, the easier it became to imagine a future without CJ. Either way, I knew one thing—Burt treated me far better than CJ did.

Burt and I became fused together, like two lost soul mates who only just realized that the thing missing in our lives had been each other all along. We hatched a plan to go to Las Vegas together to party and have some fun.

"My sister Salome won a timeshare tour in Las Vegas, and has invited me to go with her," I told CJ. "It would be such a pity to miss out on the opportunity for a free getaway. And I could use some time hanging out with her, she has been through a lot lately…"

He was convinced and allowed me to pack my things.

That weekend, Burt made a serious play for my heart. The two of us stayed at the WYNN Hotel in total luxury, and it was glam glorious.

On the Saturday evening before we were set to return home the next day, Burt spoke to me in his frank tone, "We can't keep sneaking around like this, Crystal. You need to end it with CJ. You belong with me. We could be happy together. I can give you everything—a husband, a family, and real love. Consider breaking it off with him, please."

As I went to sleep that night, I knew I would have to sit CJ down and break up with him. That meant breaking off our engagement, moving out, and starting over. I wouldn't be alone after the break-up. Burt was waiting and promising me the world.

As he lay there sleeping, I imagined a future with Burt and shivered. There was something about Burt that made me quiver. He made me feel so loved and appreciated.

Vegas streaked by in a haze of drinks, club lights, caviar, and limo rides. I felt like I regained some status with Burt, which appealed to me. Call it shallow if you want, but I was drinking Louis Roeder Cristal champagne again, and I didn't want it to ever end. Burt gave me that and more—he ticked all the boxes and offered me another shot at my ideal life.

I arrived back home on Sunday evening to a significantly agitated CJ. The first thing he noticed was the diamond watch that Burt bought me on a whim, when we were walking down the strip on Friday.

"Tell me the truth, Crystal. There is someone else, isn't there?" he asked, looking mutinous.

"What do you want me to say?" This was too soon. I was tired and not in the mood for a fight.

"How about you tell me where you really were this weekend?" CJ insisted.

I threw up my hands, defeated. "I was in Vegas."

"But not with your sister," he pushed.

"How do you know who I was with?"

"I have my sources," he barked like an angry dog. "Let's just say that someone who cares about me told me about your adventures with another man. Who is it?"

"Well you seem very well informed then. I'm sorry CJ, but it's true. We have to break-up—I've fallen in love with someone else."

For a few long moments he just stood there gaping at me like a fish. "How long has this been going on?"

"For a while. A few months maybe. I didn't mean to hurt your feelings CJ, but you know we were not working out. You're too controlling. I can't handle it."

This sent CJ spiraling into some very choice curse words and descriptions of what my lover and I can go and do together. It was a horrible break-up, as I expected. CJ forced me to recount a lot of details of my cheating, which he said would help him 'get over me.'

His ego was badly bruised. I later discovered that he was in contact with an acquaintance of mine about me. They emailed each other to discuss where I was and what I had been up to. This 'friend' of mine fed CJ information about me, and told him that my gift came from a new love interest.

His jealousy was like a self-fulfilling prophecy. From the day I fell for him he had accused me of cheating, until there was no risk anymore for me. I was already being blamed for it, so I did it.

CJ was a unique experience that added a new dimension to my experience with men and relationships. For the first time, I saw the other side of the argument. I was the one cheating, instead of the one being cheated on.

I wanted to feel bad, but I didn't. Perhaps my heart was crushed so much that it needed to find a way to back to sanity in any way that it could. I knew that my time with CJ had been short and turbulent, but passionate and exciting.

Some love relationships come on strong, but fizzle out equally as they do quickly. I was not looking for a man to convert me into some kind of slave or emotional punching bag. I was looking for a man who would see me, appreciate my tendency towards fun and freedom, and love me anyway.

CJ was a great lover, but he didn't respect my freedom. At every turn he had tried to strip me of the personality that made me who I am. He wanted to cut me off from my life and keep me in a box all to himself. I couldn't allow that to happen.

And so I learned an important lesson with CJ. That along with honesty, generosity, and someone with whom to share my life I also needed a man to respect my freedom and integrity.

I didn't consider myself a cheater. What happened with CJ and Burt was just one of those things! Once I was safe in Burt's arms, I reverted to my normal state of loyal companionship. I accepted responsibility for my actions, but didn't regret them.

Nor could I ever regret a union that gave me one of my precious children. James might have still been a young child, but he was the result of Burt and my feelings for each other.

Burt was so elated when I told him that I was pregnant! We went out to the best restaurant in the city and planned our baby's future all night. Finally, a father who wanted to be a part of his child's life. I had hit the jackpot.

Two weeks before I was due for a check-up, I collapsed. I was transported to the hospital in an ambulance due to complications with my pregnancy. It was a difficult time for Burt and me; we were worried about losing the baby.

James was impatient to be born, and he arrived at 32 weeks, very early. The hospital kept him in an incubator for two weeks before he could come home with us.

Again, I endured an emergency C section, and the drugs and procedures I endured were a trial. Luckily, Burt was there with me. He held my hand and looked after James when I couldn't. Despite all of his faults—and he did have many—Burt was always a dedicated father.

For a long moment I thought bitterly about Burt's success as a father. After all, he has been a great dad to James, and even to Jordan and Joyce! Perhaps I was too hasty in judging him. Maybe he had not been unfaithful to me, and I was just imagining things. I would have to find out the truth or it would haunt me forever.

CHAPTER 15

THE LIES PEOPLE TELL

*"Your intellect may be confused, but your emotions
will never lie to you."*

~ Roger Ebert ~

I FELL FOR BURT IN a way that I had never fallen for any man before that. He was so protective and sincere, but with a wild side that made being with him a constant adventure. I could see myself growing old with a man like that.

Even Burt's proposal was something remarkable. He booked out an entire restaurant and hired a private band to play our favorite songs. We were served a seven-course meal and when the dessert came, he pulled out a small, tasteful box with a giant diamond inside it.

Burt got down on one knee and said the words I longed to hear my entire life. "Crystal, from the moment you stepped into my life I knew I would never be the same. You have changed my heart and now it belongs to you. Will you marry me?"

It was surreal. The soft light of the restaurant shone in his eyes, as he held the box open—the perfect ring was staring back at me. I accepted. It was one of the happiest moments of my life. I felt, deep down, that Burt was my future all along.

All the men before him were just rehearsal partners for the kind of passion, mature love, and respect that we shared. It was Burt and I against the world, with James and the twins, our beautiful children. This would be my life. That was the beginning of a number of dreams that Burt manifested for me. He was very dedicated to seeing that I got everything I wanted. He was generous and wise, in a distinguished kind of way, but he could also party when he wanted to.

Burt was the ying to my yang, the crème to my coffee. All I wanted to do was please him and make him happy. We were a family, and one that worked well together. I couldn't have experienced a more heady time.

For a long time, Burt and I lived in matrimonial ecstasy. I thought that he would be mine forever, but now I wondered if forever is just a fairy-tale to help people recover from the brutal truth—that nothing truly lasts.

I sent my mother a message, telling her not to meet me. I would finish packing another day, if that was necessary. My first priority was to find out what was going on with Burt. And I needed a friend to help me through it. A friend that enjoys some alcohol!

Burt was the bomb to be married to. He took me from apartment to apartment until I fell in love with our current home. He let me decorate it and change design features. He expected me to take the advantage to make us more comfortable.

When we moved into the apartment, he kept a secret project out of the plans—my closet. It was his gift to me, out of love. What drove a man to feel such passion? How could that passion be lost so easily? Would I never understand love?

That scumbag's hoo-hoo pictures were still fresh in my mind. They made me grit my teeth and want to seek revenge. Haunted, I knew it was petty. It wasn't her fault—it was Burt's fault. I blamed him, but I loved him. I needed someone else to blame.

When Burt and I first lived together in this apartment, it was nothing short of a fairy-tale. He took the family away on regular holidays, six or seven times a year. We traveled far and wide, and more—we were good together. But Burt was also an ambitious man, driven by competition. He liked to win, as many powerful men do. He actively sought out advancement in any way that he could, with his deals, his companies, with any advantage he could get.

I wondered if Burt cheated on me because he was stressed at work. I did put pressure on him to be with his family more often. Was this some kind of twisted coping mechanism? A way to keep the fun in his life now that we settled down?

My perfect New York family was disintegrating. All because of that low-down Layaho with her uneven boobs and arrow-mole. I sat bolt upright on my closet couch, wrenched from my musings about Burt and my past life. I was a cocktail of emotions, three parts despair, two parts anger and one-part fear.

The door opened somewhere in the apartment, and I could hear Burt's voice in the distance. He must have decided to come home to face the music. Maybe if I dug a little deeper, there wouldn't be any music to face?

I zipped up my second bag, and opened a third. I wouldn't go to him; make him find me. He did. My closet-room door swung open and he stepped inside. I could tell he had enjoyed a drink or two, and he looked harassed and wild-eyed.

He settled on the white leather couch across from me, leaning deeply in my direction. "Listen, babe, we have to sort this out. I canceled my meeting. I can barely think straight with everything that has happened today."

I switched through my feelings, like an impassive game engine. Anger was the first to pop up. "Tell me the truth about those pictures, or you'll lose me," I warned.

"They don't mean anything, Crystal; why can't you believe that? You've had people stalk you, you should be more understanding about this sort of thing."

"Then why the lies, Burt? No one at the coffee shop got pictures of her tits on their phones. You lied to me. You're covering for her and that means one thing—you're cheating!" I almost shouted. In the distance, I heard another door close and remembered to keep my voice down for James's sake.

"Okay. She did send a mass text to everyone in her inbox, because she is crazy. Everyone knows she is crazy!" he pleaded with me.

"I'm not disputing her craziness, Burt; I'm trying to understand why you have been going to lunch with a crazy person who sends you full frontal pornography."

"Babe, I can't be held responsible for the actions of another person. I shouldn't have met with her, but I have not cheated on you."

"...Yet! Maybe so, but you certainly intended to with this country club slut! And what about the other pictures? I saw more than just her parts in your phone."

Burt shook his head vigorously and rested his hands on his forehead. "I can't change what you have seen. All I can do is tell you that it doesn't mean anything. I love you; I didn't cheat on you."

There it was again, that anger. Did he think I was a fool? I erupted. "I don't believe you! Do you think I'm some empty headed idiot that will believe anything you tell me just because I love you? How much do you love me, to put me through this kind of shit? This is so messed up. I thought we were happy. You made me feel like we were happy, and you were lying!"

"Don't do this, Crystal. I didn't do it. I didn't sleep with anyone else. Please don't do this," he kept saying. It only enraged me. I had seen enough cheating to know when it was happening. Burt was caught and he didn't want to admit it. It turned my stomach.

"Why do you keep lying to me? You did this. It has nothing to do with me! I've been faithful to you, which apparently was a big mistake and a total waste of time. Do you know how many times I could have cheated on you? But I never have! Now I feel like a damn idiot!" I shouted.

"Oh yeah? What about you and your ex? I see how he looks at you. You've probably been cheating on me with him for years."

"Max! Max? The other lying cheater sack of shit? That's nasty, Burt, even for you. I have no interest in being with Max ever again."

I endured enough of his lies; they were choking me. If I didn't leave, I'd be tempted to lock him in my closet, never to be seen or heard from again. I sent a hasty text to my friend Daisy, and moments later the response came.

"You're leaving now?" Burt said, his arms stretched wide.

"Yeah, Burt, imagine that. You cheat on me, and then I leave! What an unexpected consequence of your stupid decisions..." I grabbed my luggage and wheeled it to the door.

"I'm going to Daisy's this evening. The nanny will stay the night if you pay her an additional fee to look after James. Try not to sleep with her."

I slammed the door on the way out, and for a brief second felt a savage pleasure knowing I left him to his thoughts this time.

I was at Daisy's apartment less than fifteen minutes later. She already had a bottle of red wine open and Dirty Martini waiting for me—what a considerate friend. Daisy was from the Dominican Republic, and became a close friend of mine during my modeling years – we went way back. We hugged and I retold the terrible tale.

"That dog. That no good, two-timing dog." Daisy drank deeply from her glass. "How do you feel about him now?"

How did I feel? Angry of course. Disgusted. And... hurt. Sad.

My phone beeped, and text messages started.

"We are both sleep deprived. James has not been sleeping in his own bed. Do we really want to end our marriage over a misunderstanding? – Burt"

All I could do was sit there and respond, as Daisy called for some Chinese take-away.

"It's true I haven't had much sleep. But that is no excuse for your continual lying about that slut (and others?) from the fitness club. Be a man. Tell the truth! – Crystal"

"Crystal, I would never hurt you like this. I didn't cheat on you! I don't want to be with anyone but you, but you are jumping to conclusions about things. Don't let your temper get in the way of our marriage. – Burt"

Every text he sent me made me angrier. Burt was not one to text—he preferred to call and talk to someone on the phone. I knew that he was texting because he wanted to convince me he was blameless.

CHAPTER 16

THE CONFESSION

"Confession of errors is like a broom which sweeps away the dirt and leaves the surface brighter and clearer. I feel stronger for confession."

~ Mahatma Gandhi ~

THAT NIGHT I STAYED with Daisy, and she counseled me through much of the pain. By the morning, we were sharing coffee and pure outrage over Burt's behavior. Daisy had recently divorced her two-timing husband. We were two women who felt betrayed, and it made for a relaxing environment of mutual contempt.

"Women like that should to be taught a lesson," Daisy said. I could tell she was thinking about her ex-husband's floozies as much as about Burt's mistress. "Let's see. What could you do?"

The lust for vengeance coursed through my blood like strong drink. "What I want to do is embarrass her, show the whole world what a whore this Layaho is." I corrected myself. "What a whore I think she is. I'm almost certain it's her, and that she's done more than send Burt pictures of her privates, but I can't be sure. I need to know."

Daisy filled my glass with orange juice. "Are you sure you really want to know?" When I nodded vehemently, she steepled her fingers under her chin and pursed her lips. "Have you thought about asking Sheila?"

I took a minute to consider the implications of calling Sheila with whom I had partied on several occasions but never been close. Sheila worked at the country club and knew all about everything that went on there. She was a sharp-eyed observer who knew everything, saw through every pretense, detected every secret – but she was also a notorious gossip.

If anyone had observed my husband crossing boundaries, it was Sheila. But if I phoned her, she would sense a juicy scandal and spread the word among her society friends. Could I risk the humiliation and embarrassment? My need for certainty outweighed everything else.

I called.

She was helpful, sympathetic, and as eager as a cat at the sound of the can opener and the smell of tuna. I could practically hear her salivating when I told her I had discovered Burt's infidelity. She eagerly asked for details.

This was a tit-for-tat deal, and I had to provide gossip fodder to get the information I needed, so I told her about the photos. She almost purred with pleasure.

Then it was her turn to divulge what she knew. "I can tell you that Burt has been here with other women." She paused for effect. "I hate to upset you, Crystal, but..." Another pause. I gripped the phone hard, wanting her to go on. "I've seen him kissing and touching that muck face. And not just once."

I thanked her and tapped disconnect. Satisfaction and pain both churned in my chest: satisfaction because I finally knew, and because I had been right. Pain because my husband had betrayed me and I had lost the love I could trust.

Again, it felt like the floodgates of my heart opened up, and distress flooded me. Was there any end to this pain?

Daisy surveyed me quietly over her coffee.

We were sitting in her decorative lounge, the sun streaming into the large bay windows, casting us in light and warmth.

"She says, she has seen Burt kissing that woman..." I trailed off, sobbing, "More than once."

"Do you feel better now?" Daisy's voice was gentle. "Or worse?"

I felt destroyed, like someone kicked the ground out from underneath me. I was floating in space, suspended in darkness, with nothing to cling to.

It was one thing to be faced with evidence, and another to know for sure. I had solid proof now, an eyewitness that their lunches were more than just friendly meetings. If he had kissed her, it meant he had definitely lied. Yes, Burt was cheating on me.

Anger rose like acid from my stomach and bubbled through the pain. "How did you deal with it when your husband cheated and lied to you?"

"I left him." She spoke calmly, although I could hear a tremor in her voice. "And I'm recovering now. It hasn't been easy. Do you have the courage it takes to leave your man?"

"I don't want to leave him," I confessed shakily.

"Well, that's your choice. But I can tell you that if you stay the cheating will continue. Can you live with that? "

Beep. A text message.

"I'm coming over xxx – Burt"

Within an hour, Burt showed up at Daisy's door.

My heart hammered in my chest. This was it. I would hear what he wanted to say and I would decide what to do.

When Daisy showed him into the lounge, he stepped towards me with a big smile. The familiar smell of him, masculine with a hint of eucalyptus and the woody scent of his aftershave, almost made my knees melt with longing. He was wearing the blue Neiman Marcus shirt I'd given him for his birthday last year, and he looked oh-so-good in it. My head stayed cool, but my palms burned with the yearning to brush his skin, to touch his strong male jaw once more.

He carried a big bunch of red roses in his hands, which Daisy sneered at. "I'll let you two talk. If you need me, Crystal, I'll be in the other room."

And with that, Burt and I were alone in the sunlit lounge.

He sat across from me, laying the flowers down on the table and leaned forward. "Can we talk about this?"

I saw his hands – his strong, tender hands, the hands that had caressed me so many times in gentle intimacy, and forced my gaze away. "Yes, I suppose we will have to, won't we?" I tried to talk lightly, but there was croak in my voice. "How's James? Did the nanny stay?"

"Yes, she was happy to stay. I told James you needed to come to Aunt Daisy to help her."

"Good…so what is it that you want to say to me?" I pressed, a part of me desperate to catch him in more lies so that I could release my fury into the world.

"I…I love you, Crystal. I don't know what happened last night. You found some photos on my phone and the next thing I know my wife is gone. I need you to understand that I never meant to hurt you. Things have been really difficult between us lately."

I nodded, listening intently. He stared at the floor avoiding eye contact, while my eyes bored into his. "But have they been this difficult? That you turned to other women to get something you were not getting from me? I don't understand," I whispered.

"I already told you, sweetheart, I haven't done anything wrong. I didn't cheat on you with anyone! You are jumping to conclusions. Please try to see reason." I could tell that he was trying to persuade me, like one of his business meeting negotiations.

"Another lie, so this is what we have become, Burt. I'm the woman you lie to about your affairs. Well, let me tell you something I did, for my own peace of mind. Last night I called Sheila." I watched as the cogs of Burt's mind turned and landed on the name. It took him a second to realize who I meant.

"She works at the club, where your 'indiscretions' seem to originate from. And you know what she told me?" Before I spoke I saw his head fall. He was trapped now, and I was glad. "You have been seen in public kissing and touching that piece of shit who you claim sent you vagina pictures by mistake. You are a damn liar, Burt."

A tense silence permeated the lounge, and I could tell that Daisy was listening intently from the next room. You could hear nothing but our voices. Burt considered me and then he sank into a deep, defeated sigh.

"Alright. Alright, Crystal. I'm not going to lie anymore. Yes, I cheated on you with Layaho, but I never meant to hurt you." The impact of his confession hit me in the chest, sending racking sobs through my body.

"Work got crazy and every time I came home you were busy with James or in a bad mood…I know, I know your grandmother just passed… what I mean is that I needed to do something to feel good about myself… for work…"

At his selfish confession my heart went cold. I stood up and gathered myself as best I could. "Thank you for telling the truth. Our marriage is over. I want a divorce. I can't have my children growing up in a house where their father thinks cheating is okay. You've lost your mind."

Then, Burt feigned confusion. "What do you mean you're leaving me? A divorce? You cannot leave! If you stay with me, we can fix this."

"No. We can't."

Just then Daisy bustled back into the room, on cue. "I'm sorry, did I interrupt something?"

"Burt was just leaving. I've said all I have to say to him right now."

Burt looked confused, crestfallen—like he never imagined a scenario that would lead to me leaving him. What did he expect? That I would stay with him because of his amazing persuasion? No amount could buy his way out of this kind of betrayal.

As Burt was floundering and trying to continue the conversation, Daisy started shunting him towards the door. "Hey, let me talk to my wife," he insisted as she ushered him backwards.

"It is over now. Burt, you understand? You destroyed your marriage with that woman. I hope it was worth it." Daisy opened the front door. "Now get out."

Burt made one final lunge to get back into the house, but Daisy stuck out her foot and he tumbled over it on the floor in the doorway. "That's enough now. You gather yourself and go home. Both of you have a lot of change coming."

She slammed the door in his face and came to sit with me. "You'll be okay, Crystal. You'll rebuild. He is the one that lost something today. And he will soon realize it."

"My marriage is over," I said sadly.

"Yes, but that means you can make room for a life of your own."

Once I recovered from Burt's visit, Daisy decided to open another bottle of wine. It seemed to make everything better and helped me say nasty things about Burt. "Nice legwork," I said to Daisy on our third glass. "I don't think he's ever been tripped before."

She raised her glass. "One indignity deserves another."

Burt was always the kind of man to get back up, just as he had done in the doorway. I felt a real sense of loss then, for the man who had loved me once. Somehow his love had eroded over time, and a sense of entitlement crept in.

"He needed to be happy…" I repeated. "That scum bag!"

CHAPTER 17

LEAVING DAISY

"Friendship... is not something you learn in school.
But if you haven't learned the meaning of friendship,
you really haven't learned anything."

~ Muhammad Ali ~

THAT NIGHT DAISY AND I drank twice as much as the night before. In all of our glorious wisdom, we laughed at and mocked the men who turned from us. It made me feel a little better.

"Why did he deny everything for so long?" Daisy sipped wine. "Once you discovered those pictures, his only chance to win your trust back was to come clean and admit everything. Was he too stupid to realize that?"

"I know, right." My drunken mind leaped to the images. "You can see it's the same uneven pair, with the left boob lower and bigger than the right, and that mole shaped like an arrow. What kind of puta has to take photos of herself like this? Even a porn site would reject those uneven boobs."

Fueled by alcohol and fury, I pulled my laptop onto my lap, and with a few clicks I posted the disgusting pictures on Facebook.

"What are you doing?" Daisy leaned to look at the screen, and clapped a hand over her mouth. "Crystal! Are you sure this is wise?"

"Oh yes!" I declared. "The whole world shall see what a slut she is!" I kept going, until every single photo was uploaded, with captions like 'Home wrecker!' and 'Slimy slut!'

Sure enough, about a half an hour later the first 'like' appeared below the images. My triumph was short-lived. It was Burt.

"That son of a bitch has liked her photos again!" I fumed.

Daisy studied me gravely. "What did you expect him to do?"

"Learn a lesson! Everyone will see these pictures and know what a lying, cheating bastard he is."

"Maybe." She was rubbing her chin. "I've never used Facebook. Are you sure this is how it works?"

"Yes. Facebook is great for exposing nasty bastards. The pictures may even go viral, and then –" I came to a halt and blinked. Had someone just unfriended me?

I put my glass down. "Someone has taken her side over mine!"

Daisy refilled both our glasses. "That was to be expected, wasn't it?"

While Daisy dozed on the coach, I checked Facebook again... More people had unfriended me – not just people who knew Burt in real life and might take his side, but online acquaintances from my own circles who owed him no loyalty.

I scrounged around Daisy's kitchen on the hunt for more wine.

She woke with a start, and kicked off the couch throw I covered her with. "Why are you not sleeping, Crystal?"

"Can't sleep, need more wine," I muttered drunkenly. For the last hour or so notifications kept coming in hard and fast—people were un-friending me on Facebook.

"There isn't any more. I can get some later on. Are you okay?"

"No...no, I'm not okay. I thought Carla and Michelle were my friends, but they have both unfriended me on Facebook. It's Burt, he's turning them all against me!" I cried.

She pushed me into the seat. "Are you sure that's what's happening?"

"I'm going to call Lisa and ask her why she unfriended me."

"Are you sure that's a good idea?" She sat down beside me and held my wrist. "I don't understand Facebook. How do people normally react when someone posts naked boobs on their wall or their timeline or whatever it's called? Do they welcome this sort of thing?"

"No, not normally, but..." I paused.

Normally, people blocked the sender. That's what I habitually did with offensive content. Whenever someone spammed me, posted explicit pictures or made bitchy comments, I hit the 'unfriend' button.

Of course, this was different. These pictures were posted for a reason.

But what if my Facebook friends didn't see it that way? All they saw was a series of lewd photos and bitchy posts. Of course they were displeased. They might even have received those images on the screen in their workplace, or with their children around.

But the captions showed that I was the injured party, posting in self-defense, didn't they? Unfortunately, they also showed me as an immature, vengeful, childish bitch.

As this realization sank in, regret took hold. What a stupid thing I had done! The heat of shame flooded my face.

Hastily, I hit *delete-delete-delete*. But it was too late to undo the damage. Too many people had already seen the posts, and many more would soon see them because they were already delivered to their devices.

I had to send another post, apologizing, explaining that I was drunk. But the people who had unfriended me would no longer see it. And what could I say, anyway? I couldn't claim it was a drunken joke of no consequence, because that would imply nothing had happened.

My head pounded with the effort of thinking, and ugly tension knotted the back of my neck. I would postpone my next Facebook post until I was sober and could come up with a sane strategy for damage limitation.

I had lost not just my husband, but my friends – not because of their divided loyalties, but because of my own choices. I had tried to use my friends for my personal vengeance, and caused them embarrassment.

I settled down for the night, but sleep eluded me for a long time as uninvited insights knocked and demanded admission.

Those thoughtless Facebook posts were not even a one-time drunken mistake. Rather, they were typical for how I treated friends: selfishly, without consideration for their needs.

I used friends when it suited me, and discarded them when they lost their value. Small wonder they didn't give me their full loyalty. I recalled incident after incident, and although I tried to chase those memories away, they clung.

I remembered the bitching, disloyal behavior of my so-called friends around the time of my wedding to Max. At the time, I had resented their resentment, and decided they were simply not real friends. But had I been a better friend to them? Had I genuinely cared about their concerns, rejoiced in their fortunes, supported their goals? I had been too absorbed in my own life to pay attention to what was going on theirs.

What about all the friends I had made in high school, in the music company, in the bars where I waitressed, in modeling, in finance? I had faded into and out of their lives. This wasn't due to lack of effort on their part, but sheer self-absorption on mine.

But I did have real friends, didn't I? People with whom I went back a long time. People like Daisy, who were there for me when I needed them.

Cold insight washed through me. When Daisy's marriage broke up, I hadn't been there for her to lend support. She'd phoned me once or twice, had even asked if I could come and stay, but I had been too busy. Yet now when I needed her, she was there for me.

The uncomfortable insights didn't stop. Had I been a better lover than a friend, or had I taken my men for granted, used them when it suited me, and discarded them when they were no longer a good fit? Had I been so self-absorbed that I didn't understand their needs, didn't see what was going on in their lives?

Burt hadn't been happy in our marriage for months, and I hadn't even noticed. I'd hated Max for cheating on me, but I had done exactly the same to CJ, caring little about the hurt I caused. I'd resented men for not giving me honesty and respect – but I dumped Tad who had given me both.

More and more insights came rushing into my head, tormenting me until I tossed and turned with guilt and pain.

The next morning, I felt better, and I put last night's insights away.

It was easier to focus on what Burt had done wrong, and learn the superficial lessons that didn't involve changing myself.

CHAPTER 18

GOING HOME

*"Love begins at home, and it is not how much we do...
but how much love we put in that action."*

~ Mother Teresa ~

THE DOOR SWUNG OPEN in my old childhood home in Long Island, and I stepped inside. The familiar smells of mothballs, furniture polish and freshly baked bread wrapped around me. A hug from my mother, then another from my father greeted me. The twins were with their father, and so was James; for now! I was home.

My mother put on a pot of tea, and we settled around the dining room table. I left my luggage at the door, five brimming Dolce & Gabbana leopard print suitcases. I had squeezed all of the possessions I could carry into these bags, along with my former life with Burt.

The tea felt warm in my hands. A cool certainty settled on me like a fine silk veil. I knew I was safe here, and that I could stay as long as I needed to get back on my feet.

"Strange being back here after all these years," I mused.

My father eyed me anxiously. "Are you okay, daughter, what can we do to help you?"

"You're already doing it." I attempted a smile. "I'm sorry to barge in on you like this. I wasn't planning to be back here…after everything."

My mother reached out and took my hand. "Don't you worry about any of that. You know you're always welcome with us." She shot a warning glance at my father.

As much as I loved him, I knew he wanted to ask me if I'd be contributing to the household finances.

Of course I couldn't expect them to take on the expense of having me living with them, but now was not the time to discuss the details.

Both my mother and my father were acutely aware that I had just fallen from a life of economic changes— and not for the first time. After another quiet moment my father perked up. "When I get my hands on that husband of yours, I'm going to choke the fidelity back into him."

"I appreciate that, Dad, but I don't want him back. We are over now… for good." My voice rang through the old linoleum kitchen. "I've asked for a divorce."

My mother frowned for me. "Oh no, Crystal, is it that bad? No reconciliation at all?"

I drew in a deep, steadying breath. "Don't think so. He has been cheating on me for longer than I want anyone to know. I can't stay married to a man like that. Perhaps best for both of us if he is free to be with whomever he wants, and I am free to pursue my own happiness."

It was a rehearsed answer, and it came out better than I expected. But I could see from my parents' faces that I wasn't fooling them. I finished my tea and said my excuses. It would be the first night back in my childhood home since I was a teenager, and as an adult I felt an exhaustion that comes from the inexplicable ache of age and regret.

"I'm off to bed now. Thank you for letting me stay here, I'm sure I will be better company in the morning." It took me three trips to carry my luggage down into the basement, where my mother and father had made room for me.

It was clean and dry down there, with a single bed and some storage space—but the light was artificial. I felt like I was locked away in a dungeon, and that it was my own fault. Of all the men that I was in love with, Burt had come as the biggest surprise.

I had never been a naive adult. But I had believed Burt was different, perhaps for my own selfish reasons. He seemed so sincere. The truth was that he had chosen to step out on the marriage at the beginning of the year already.

He had grown so distant from me since James was born. I looked after him all the time, and there were demands with the twins and their father too. I guess in the end…Burt always assumed the worst because of his insecurities and misbehaving. I remained faithful to our family.

Regardless of my circumstances, I knew that life had thrown yet another challenge at me. The fates were trying to tell me something important this time. I had to open my heart and listen, really listen—to end this cycle of heartache and abuse.

No, not the kind of abuse that came with a cheating husband – the kind that came when you didn't etch out a life for yourself in the world, when you readily accepted the life of another and pretended it was your own.

It took some time unpacking a few things and reflecting on the mess I had gotten myself into. Today was the first day of the rest of my life. Aha! How cliché? What would I become? What would happen to me? Only I could decide my future.

"Dinner!" came a voice from upstairs. My stomach rumbled in response. I bounded up the many stairs to the landing above the basement, trying not to feel like a failure. When I reached the doorway and crossed into the kitchen, I froze.

There, was my entire family—my mother and father, and all nine of my siblings. My sisters with each of their husbands, and my brothers, with their spouses. They smiled as I entered. "Crystal! Thought we would get together for an excellent dinner," mom said innocently.

I knew what mom was trying to do, and I appreciated it. My mom and Daisy had a relatively close relationship. Her mom and mine were long time church group friends. I suspected Daisy told my mom that I felt really alone since this tragic ordeal.

I hugged everyone and delighted in being offered a chair at the head of the table, a position reserved exclusively for my father. "You need it more than me today. And why sit when you can stand!" my dad exclaimed, "That chair kills my back."

Thankfully no one brought up B-liar or the monstrous vagina pictures that I made so public. It was like it never happened. My siblings and family distracted me with news from their lives, good news—and they asked me what was in the cards for me in the coming months.

"Not a clue, haven't figured it out just yet," I admitted between mouthfuls of curry chicken. "Probably something on my own time. Rebuild. Research and utilize time and resources wisely."

"Wise words." My father lifted his glass. "And bear in mind that you can't change other people, but you can change yourself." I saw in his dark eyes something he would not say, but I understood the message nevertheless: it was time that I changed myself.

Together we feasted on a simple meal of chicken, rice and peas that gave me more strength than any I had eaten in a five-star restaurant. My family would always be here for me, and that was something priceless. Once again, I felt like the feisty 18-year-old model with the world at my feet.

That night I retired to the charming basement full of wonder. I had been in love, out of love, up then down, then up again. I had felt passion and been on the wrong side of an affair, and I had felt the keen sting of betrayal.

All I could do sitting on the white cotton covers was smile. Hope bloomed in my heart like a mighty flower. It was funny how the men I loved taught me so many things. With Barry I believed that honesty was the key to a good relationship, with Tad I realized the importance of financial stability and ambition.

When I met Max all I wanted was closeness and someone to spend my life with—someone that wouldn't treat me like an extension of their wealth, like an object. The chaos of his love drove me into the arms of CJ, the control-freak.

Once again I was in love with a man who took something from me, *my freedom*. That was when I realized I couldn't live without my integrity and personal liberty intact. And then Burt, quite suddenly, became another lesson.

For a long time, I believed that Burt was the culmination of the lessons I learned about men in my life. He was tactfully honest and dutiful, kept me close but allowed me my freedom and all the ambition I could ever want.

There was just one problem. Burt was loyal to himself first. He confessed it that day at Daisy's apartment. When he felt his world crashing down around him, he broke his vows to regain his happiness. I could never imagine doing that to my husband. Yet, a part of me still loved him.

Sitting there with my piles of designer clothing on the bare, tiled floor, I realized what a sharp change this would be for me. A necessary change. Some people figure out who they are when they are very young, others—like me, are still work in progress.

It took me five relationships to realize that the traits I valued most, I needed to cherish and nurture inside myself first. Of course I wanted to see them in the man I fell for. But mostly I wanted to be with someone who believed in trust the same as I believed. I needed time to heal.

EPILOGUE

I DON'T REGRET THE THINGS in life I can't change. I don't know what's going to happen with my marriage, and how it will affect the children, but I won't ever let a man have such financial, emotional and spiritual control over me ever again.

As a first step, I'll dust off my degree, licenses and skills, and look for a job in finance.

I'll learn to be a better friend, and stop taking everyone's attention and support for granted.

I'm capable of learning. After learning five lessons about five men, it's time that I learn about myself.

Instead of pinning my hopes for happiness on one man after another, and despairing when he doesn't measure up to what I want, I'll grow into the person I'm meant to be.

The child Crystal, attention-seeking, superficial and chasing after everything that glittered, has gone. The real Crystal, the woman of depth and inner strength, is emerging from the dark. I can't see her fully yet, but I think I'll like her. Life with her will be different, but I know we will have fun.

DEAR READER,

DID YOU ENJOY THIS book? I'd love it if you could post a review on Amazon (*www.amazon.com/author/daprince*), saying which parts you liked best.

If you want to ask me a question, drop me a line. Also let me know if you've spotted any typos, so I can correct them in the next edition. I enjoy hearing from readers.

My email is *Deann.Prince@aol.com*.

You can also visit my website *Deannprince.com*, and follow me on Twitter *twitter.com/D_A_Prince_* and if you tweet me *@D_A_Prince_* that you've read this book, I'll probably follow you back.

I look forward to hearing from you.

D.A. Prince

ABOUT THE AUTHOR

 D.A. Prince has worked as a dept store cosmetic salesperson, fashion model, skip tracer, voice-over actor and owned a juice bar cafe.

A native New Yorker, she now lives with her husband and sons in Palm Beach, Florida, close enough to the ocean to hear the waves at night. She is a soccer mum who enjoys travel, tennis, dancing, and listening to reggae, R&B and soul.

Her idea of bliss is dining with her husband in a restaurant where tuxedoed waiters attend to their every whim and silver cutlery clinks on bone china plates, savoring stone crabs, lobster tails, creamed asparagus and potato chips with a bottle of Benoit Gautier Vouvray.

REFERENCES

de La Rochefoucauld. Francois, Quotes, *http://www.brainyquote.com/ quotes/quotes/f/francoisde106547.html*

Hale, Mandy, Quotes, *http://www.goodreads.com/quotes/862014- sometimes-it-takes-a-heartbreak-to-shake-us-awake*

Clinton, William, J, Quotes. *http://www.brainyquote.com/quotes/ quotes/w/williaCJc454937.html*

Schroder, Ricky, Quotes, *http://www.brainyquote.com/quotes/quotes/r/ rickyschro503981.html*

Webb, Veronica, Quotes, *http://www.brainyquote.com/quotes/quotes/v/ veronicawe536499.html*

Jones, Rashida, Quotes, *http://www.brainyquote.com/quotes/quotes/r/ rashidajon491749.html*

Humphrey, Hubert, H, Quotes, *http://www.brainyquote.com/quotes/ quotes/h/huberthhu398405.html*

West, Mae, Quotes, *http://www.brainyquote.com/quotes/quotes/m/ maewest125640.html*

Quote Investigator, Love Set Free, *http://quoteinvestigator. com/2012/04/08/love-set-free/*

Grohl, Dave, Quotes, *http://www.brainyquote.com/quotes/quotes/d/davegrohl418219.html*

Dunst, Kirsten, Quotes, *http://www.brainyquote.com/quotes/quotes/k/kirstendun401285.html*

Hathaway, Anne, Quotes, *http://www.brainyquote.com/quotes/quotes/a/annehathaw443627.html*

Kent, Germany, Quotes, *https://www.goodreads.com/author/quotes/8557658.Germany_Kent*

Cheating Quotes, *http://www.brainyquote.com/quotes/keywords/cheating.html*

Lie Quotes, *http://www.brainyquote.com/quotes/keywords/lie.html*

Confession Quotes, *http://www.brainyquote.com/quotes/keywords/confession.html*

Friendship Quotes, *http://www.brainyquote.com/quotes/topics/topic_friendship.html*

Home Quotes, *http://www.brainyquote.com/quotes/topics/topic_home.html*